Saskatoon
A Century in Pictures

Saskatoon
A Century in Pictures

William P. Delainey
John D. Duerkop
William A. S. Sarjeant

Western Producer Prairie Books
Saskatoon, Saskatchewan

Western Producer Prairie Books
Saskatoon, Saskatchewan

Cover and book design by Craig Romanyk

The publisher acknowledges support of this publication by the Potash Corporation of Saskatchewan.

Printed and bound in Canada
by Modern Press 1
Saskatoon, Saskatchewan

Western Producer Prairie Books publications are produced and manufactured in the middle of western Canada by a unique publishing venture owned by a group of prairie farmers who are members of Saskatchewan Wheat Pool. From the first book in 1954, a reprint of a serial originally carried in the weekly newpaper, *The Western Producer,* to the book before you now, the tradition of providing enjoyable and informative reading for all Canadians is continued.

Canadian Cataloguing in Publication Data

Delainey, William T., 1942-
   Saskatoon, a Century in pictures

      Includes index.
      ISBN 0-88833-090-1 (bound). — ISBN
0-88833-089-8 (pbk.)

      1. Saskatoon (Sask.) — Description — Views.
2. Saskatoon (Sask.)) History. I. Duerkop,
John, 1944- II. Sarjeant, William Antony S.,
1935- III. Title.
FC3547.37.D44   971.24'2   C82-091235-2
F1074.5.S3D44

Contents

=Acknowledgments=

In the preparation of this work, we received help from many persons, to all of whom we are deeply indebted. In particular, its production would not have been possible without the support of the Saskatoon Public Library, the Saskatchewan Archives, and the Saskatoon *Star-Phoenix*; their generous permission to reproduce photographs has been crucial. We would like to make special mention also of the assistance received from Wilbur Lepp, June Colvine, Julie Harris, and Brock Silversides (Local History Department, Saskatoon Public Library); Ian Wilson, Lloyd Rodwell, and D'Arcy Hande (Saskatchewan Archives). Stan Hanson (university archivist, University of Saskatchewan) kindly read and criticized the manuscript.

These are, however, only some of the names in the long list of persons who assisted us. All of the following either furnished photographs for consideration for inclusion, provided us with valuable information, or helped in the production of this work. To each we extend our sincere thanks:

Brian Bachewich (Cairns Homes); John Bradley (Delmar Studios Ltd.); Joan Champ (Western Development Museum); Ray Crone of Regina; Robin Currie (Audio-Visual Services, University of Saskatchewan); Tony Dagnone (University Hospital and Century Saskatoon); Doug Eagle; Jim Ellis (Department of Soil Sciences, University of Saskatchewan); Dennis Fisher (CFQC Radio); Murray Gibson; Marion Graham; Mel Hepburn; Bill Jack (Royal Canadian Legion #63); Marie Kischuk and Albert Kitzkowski (Ukrainian Museum of Canada); Eldy Kolbussen (Arena rink); Ron Koroll (Modern Press); Linda Krukewich and Dagmar Pearson (research assistants to W.A.S. Sarjeant); Dr. Walter O. Kupsch (Department of Geological Sciences, University of Saskatchewan); Mrs. D. E. Mallough; René Marleau (Parks and Recreation Board, City of Saskatoon); Hugh McElligott (Air Canada); the Meewasin Valley Authority; Al Meyers (Meyers Construction); Don Perkins (*Star-Phoenix* Library); Norm Robson; E. T. (Pete) Russell; Lyle Sanderson and Val Schneider (College of Physical Education, University of Saskatchewan); Ed Sebestyen; Lieut.-Colonel E. Seneshen (Hugh Cairns V.C. Armories); John Smyth; Dr. Jack Summers (College of Pharmacy, University of Saskatchewan); Andras Tahn (25th Street Theatre); Rich Van Impe (Saskatoon Golf and Country Club); Neil Wagner; Dr. Ernest Walker (Department of Anthropology and Archaeology, University of Saskatchewan); Easten Wayman; Patricia Williams (Diefenbaker Centre, University of Saskatchewan); Joe Young (El-Rancho Food Services Limited); and Joe Zeman. Specific photo credits are given separately.

The publication of this book might not have been possible without the financial support of the Potash Corporation of Saskatchewan and the enthusiastic endorsement of Century Saskatoon.

Finally, we would like to express appreciation to our wives — Dawn Delainey, Diana Duerkop, and A. Margaret Sarjeant — for their support, direct and indirect, during our work on this book and throughout our lives together.

Chapter 1
The Centuries before Saskatoon (to 1882)

The Setting

In much of central Saskatchewan, the solid rocks are buried deep beneath what is indeed a young landscape. At the beginning of the great ice age, only two million or so years ago, huge glaciers advanced from the north into this region. The ice was laden with debris, fragments of all sizes from great boulders to fine rock powder. The climate was not uniformly cold during those times. During phases when the ice melted and the ice front retreated, coarse debris was deposited to form moraine ridges, and finer fragments were carried south by meltwaters to spread out and settle in temporary lakes. Then would come a colder phase, new surges of ice gouging deep channels into the sediment and by-passing or thrusting through the boulder ridges. During the last retreat of the glaciers, 12,000 years ago, the melting ice dropped all of its debris and the meltwaters transported it, spread it, and moulded it anew.

The result was a landscape that is far from monotonous, though without dramatic topography. The ice retreat was discontinuous, piecemeal. Where ice masses stagnated and ultimately melted, there are hollows occupied now by sloughs or marshes. Hummocky, rock-strewn ridges mark positions where ice fronts stood still, and empty valleys or coulees remain where meltwater streams once flowed. There are broad stretches of cohesive clays and silts forming rich soils; elsewhere, sands from the margins of dried-out lakes have been banked up and shifted by winds to form dunes.

For indeed, it became a relatively arid region. The mountain barriers of the Rockies blocked the passage of moderating air masses. The ice sheets had retreated, but the winters remained long and cold, though they brought little snow. Spring was a brief season, its rains unpredictable; the summers were always dry. Only one great river system remained, fed by residual ice and snow in the mountains. Once it had flowed fast and cut a broad channel; now the Saskatchewan was shallower and slower-flowing, meandering and leaving half-moon-shaped lakes —

Pike Lake, Moon Lake — slowly to dry out where its channels had once been. Alongside its waters, terraces remained to show where the river level once had stood.

The Wandering Tribes

A thousand years after the ice had gone, the Saskatoon region was one of true prairie. The river valleys and sheltered coulees carried the best growth of grasses and shrubs, staying green longest in the summer. They were a haven for wild life, especially for the buffalo herds that migrated continually in search of pasture. When tribes of humans first entered the region in their own ceaseless quest for food, it was to these same river valleys that they came.

When did they first arrive? Finds of stone artifacts suggest they were here 10,000 years ago, perhaps hunting for mammoths. Certainly they were here 6,000 years ago, for two of their campsites by the South Saskatchewan — the Gowen sites on the southwestern edge of Saskatoon — have been excavated. It was a hot, arid period and the people were having a hard fight for survival. Broken stone tools were reshaped and reused repeatedly; bones were laboriously crushed and split to extract the last vestiges of marrow.

Yet having arrived, these people stayed. Their way of life was already based almost entirely on the buffalo, and it remained so after a climatic shift 5,000 years ago changed the region to one of aspen parkland. The buffalo provided not only food but also clothing, shelter, ornaments, and tools. For more than 6,000 years, the Indians followed the herds on foot. They carried their possessions, for the first horses did not appear on the Great Plains till the sixteenth century A.D.

Though nomads, the hunting tribes returned again and again to a favorable campsite where there was shelter and good water, Tipperary Creek, for example, where they constructed a medicine wheel for their religious ceremonies. The people were a part of the landscape; they did not destroy it or even alter it perceptibly. When the white settlers came, the land was much the same as it had been when the Indians had come, so many thousand years earlier.

The First European Contacts

The Hudson's Bay Company claimed this region as part of its trade hinterland in 1670 and sent men like Henry Kelsey and Anthony Henday on preliminary explorations. The Saskatchewan River became a highway for the fur trade, but though many trading posts were built along the North Saskatchewan, there were few on the South branch. Instead, for almost two centuries, the contact of the native peoples with European culture was to be indirect, through their "half-brothers" the Métis. After Manitoba was proclaimed a province in 1870, large numbers of Métis forsook that region and retreated farther west to maintain their own way of life. They chose land along the banks of the Saskatchewan, cropping small acreages and establishing permanent communities like Batoche and St. Laurent. Annually they would hunt the buffalo for hides and pemmican to trade at the Company posts.

By the 1880s this movement between settlements and trading posts had produced a system of rutted trails across the prairie. In the dry summers, clouds of dust raised by the passage of squeaking Red River carts drawn by oxen were becoming a common sight.

Prelude to Colonization

As early as late 1850s, both the British and Canadian governments began considering the prospects for settlement of the prairies. Two expeditions were dispatched to explore the region. The Royal Geographical Society sent six men under Captain John Palliser; the Canadian government, a party of similar size whose most important members were surveyor S. J. Dawson and geologist Henry Youle Hind. Though both parties were dubious about prospects in the lands just north of the United States border, they agreed about the likely fertility of the parklands. Hind sketched onto his maps a "fertile belt" which included part of the South Saskatchewan valley east of the Eagle Hills, the area destined to be the site of Saskatoon.

However, the Hudson's Bay Company viewed settlement with disfavor; nothing could be done until its control was taken away in 1870 by the Canadian government of John A. Macdonald. The region became part of what was called the Northwest Territories. The land was soon being surveyed into mile-square sections; the North West Mounted Police were establishing their control; and by 1881 a transcontinental railroad was under construction.

By then, the buffalo had been hunted almost to extinction. Their traditional way of life destroyed, the native tribes were persuaded to restrict their movements to small "reservations" of land, in return for aid from the Canadian government. In the South Saskatchewan valley, Cree reserves were designated close to the Métis settlements in the north, while a group of Sioux from the United States were allocated land in the Moose Woods area to the south. A telegraph line now traversed the prairies, crossing the river just north of Saskatoon at the same point as a branch of the Carlton Trail. Here John F. Clark, the first homesteader in the region, established the first ferry service at Clark's Crossing in 1881. Settlement in the Saskatoon region had begun.

Scene at the Gowen sites in the city dump south of Saskatoon in 1977 and 1979. Members of an archaeological team carefully removed overburden to study campsites of early man. These sites were named after Charlie Gowen, the bulldozer operator who first uncovered them.

The ceremonial center or *medicine wheel* at Tipperary Creek, north of the city. The find was mapped in detail between 1959 and 1964, when this picture was taken. This wheel, with the characteristic concentration of stones in the center of the ring, may be the farthest north of its kind on the continent.

Tepee rings, formed where the stones used to hold down the bottom of a tepee rolled away when it was taken down. Usually they remained in a rough circle, and some, like this one close to Tipperary Creek, still may be seen today.

Evidence that during the fur trade era the native peoples of the prairies experienced rapid cultural and economic changes. These pictures show Red River carts, tin pails, trade cloth and clothing, crockery, and other indications of contact with whites.

Chapter 2
The Temperance Colony Era (1882 · 1903)

Though it had begun, settlement of the prairies proceeded slowly despite the offer of free homesteads — too slowly in the view of the Dominion government. Accordingly the Homestead Act was amended in 1881; colonization companies might now obtain large land grants, on the condition that the land be settled quickly. Toronto businessman J. A. Livingston perceived an opportunity to make money. He and John Lake, a stockbroker and former Methodist minister, formulated a scheme for a temperance colony in the West where a way of life free from the evils of alcohol might be fostered. With the support of members of the Temperance Society of Toronto, a colonization company was formed and a massive land grant applied for. Only a part of the land solicited was obtained, but it was nevertheless sizeable — twenty-one townships astride the South Saskatchewan River between the Moose Woods and Clark's Crossing. Advertising was begun for families to settle "where they will be ever free from the accursed influence of the liquor traffic" in a land of "prosperity, peace, and plenty."

Early in the spring of 1882, John Lake, now commissioner of the Temperance Colonization Society, travelled with an advance party by rail to the end of the tracks at Moosomin and then onward by wagon to examine the grant of land and choose the site for an administrative center. A trek along the river convinced them that there was only one point where the banks on both sides were low enough to provide an easy crossing. Lake chose the elevated area directly to the east of the crossing as the future town site. Initially he considered calling it *Minnetonka*; but when a companion brought him some delicious berries picked from shrubs growing on the river bank, he was told the native name for them was *Mis-sask-quah-too-men*. Accordingly, or so he claimed later, Lake looked out over the site and intoned: "Arise, Saskatoon, Queen of the North!"

The following spring brought the first settlers, travelling overland from the new railhead at Moose Jaw. The town site was laid out with wide streets which, it was hoped, would someday have tree-lined boulevards. A ferry was established and the first

dwellings were erected: Society offices, a blacksmith shop, a sawmill, and, eventually, a little stone schoolhouse. The Temperance Colony Pioneers' Society provided literary entertainment and practical information, serving as a forerunner of the numerous community interest groups that were to achieve so much in the life of the city. It sponsored the first newspaper, the *Sentinel* (written out in longhand); it operated the ferry; and it established the Pioneer Cemetery. Its successor, the Central Saskatchewan Agricultural Society, sponsored the first agricultural fair in 1887 at the Louise grounds where Nutana Collegiate is located today. From the outset Saskatoon was a strongly religious community. As early as 1884, a Methodist minister was appointed to a new circuit centered on the colony.

The little hamlet achieved a temporary renown during the Riel Rebellion of 1885, when it was used as a staging post and field hospital for General Middleton's troops. Some cattlemen were attracted to the lush meadow lands about Pike Lake and Moon Lake. By 1888 Saskatoon could boast twelve business establishments, including three general stores, a brick hotel, a dressmaker, a tinsmith, a post office, and a physician. Yet in general, the five years that followed the rebellion were ones of drought and early frost, hard work, poor crops, and isolation. The steamboat service failed, in part because of financial problems, in part because of the difficulties of navigation on a shallow river with so many shifting sandbanks.

Then, in 1890, circumstances changed abruptly. The Qu'Appelle, Long Lake, and Saskatchewan Railroad, building north to Prince Albert from the main Canadian Pacific Railway line, crossed the river at Saskatoon and ended the isolation. Had the tracks gone elsewhere, the settlement might well have withered away.

Initial enthusiasm at the coming of the railway was dampened when the railway company decided to locate its station, not on the high eastern bank, but on the low western bank of the river where there was easier access to a water supply for the locomotives. A new town site was surveyed, focused on the station.

The streets, laid out by the Temperance Colonization Company, were wide, and the river bank was reserved for possible steamboat traffic — fortunately for posterity. Wood-frame and stone hotels and stores sprang up, along with new dwellings and a new school.

The settlers on the east bank felt cut off, for the ferry service was infrequent and the hike across the high railway trestle was a dangerous business. The original settlement languished. When the post office shifted across the river, the west bank settlement took over the name "Saskatoon." The east bank settlement came instead to be called "Nutana," claimed to mean "first born" in Cree but more likely just a scrambled inversion of Saskatoon.

As shipments of buffalo bones, cattle, and grain began to move out of the region and as settlers and goods moved in, a commercial area arose on the land just west of the railway tracks. Here the Battleford and Bone trails came together at the railroad station. Men of enterprise — shopkeepers, newspapermen, real estate dealers, entrepreneurs of all types — were attracted to the settlement. A shift from the temperance colony concept of a western utopia free from eastern vices became apparent by the end of the century, for the first break and entry case was reported; the first bar opened; and there was a demand that commercial ventures be allowed to operate on Sundays!

Long before then, the Temperance Colonization Society had become embroiled in a flurry of court cases over what its scripholders believed had been misrepresentations. It had incorporated as a company in 1882, receiving 213,000 acres of land, but by 1891 its grant had been cancelled. However, the "bright ideal" had not quite faded away, and the region long retained a strong temperance lobby.

At the turn of the century, Saskatoon was disdainfully described by a Regina newspaper of that time as merely "a universal array of shacks." Nevertheless, the rate and extent of growth on the west bank was beyond the scope of voluntary financing and control. Improved street maintenance, refuse disposal, health and building regulations, and policing were necessary. In 1901, the residents of the new Saskatoon requested and received the right to incorporate as a village, and in 1903 it became a town.

The east bank settlement remained isolated from this growth and the problems it brought. Voluntary services still sufficed and Nutana remained a hamlet.

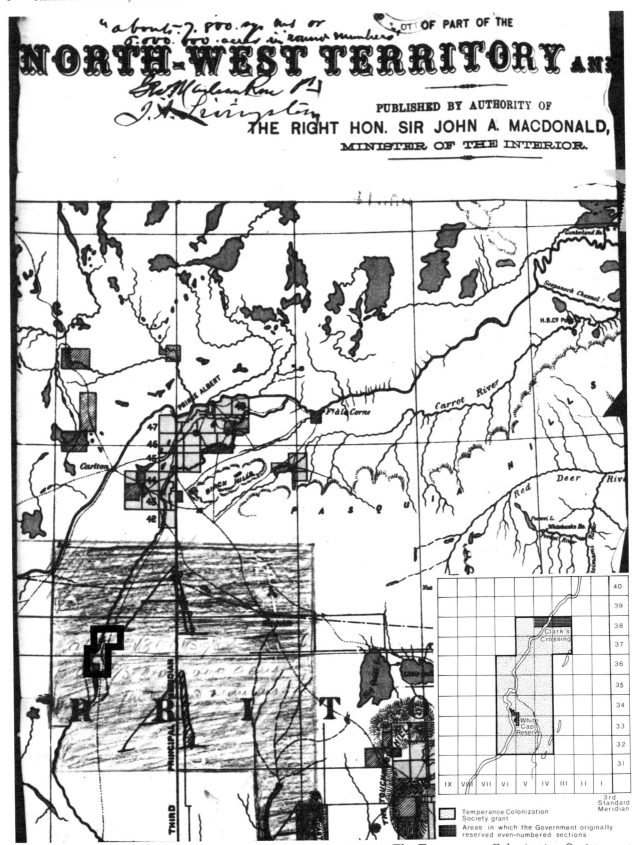

Crayoned map forwarded to the Department of the Interior in 1881. The Temperance Colonization Society sent it to show the land they would like to have included in their grant. The insert in the bottom right-hand corner corresponds to the area outlined in black within the shaded portion of the map and shows the land grant they received.

John Lake, founder of Saskatoon.

Chief White Cap, whose band of Sioux fled from Minnesota during the spring of 1862 and settled on the reserve south of Saskatoon. White Cap advised John Lake's party that the best place to cross the river was at Section 29, where Saskatoon stands today.

One of the ads which the Temperance Colonization Society placed in newspapers across Canada, hoping to attract like-minded settlers.

Sketch of Saskatoon drawn in 1885 during the Northwest Rebellion. Judging from the configuration of the ferry cable, the water is flowing the wrong way! The house in the foreground on the left is still standing; it is now 326 Eleventh Street.

The Pioneer Cemetery on the bank of the river just west of the present exhibition grounds, established in 1882. The site was chosen to bury Robert Clark, who died while fighting a prairie fire on the first day he arrived in the settlement. Edward Meeres froze to death when he became lost in a blizzard after leaving a house near Broadway Avenue and Tenth Street to go to his barn a short distance away.

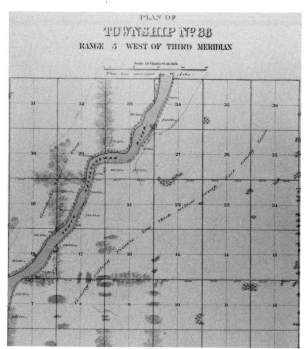

The original survey map of Township 36, Range 5, West of the Third Meridian as printed by the government in 1884. The survey, made in 1882, showed nothing altered by human beings except a few wagon trails.

The first issue of *The Saskatoon Sentinel*. One of the extracurricular activities of the teacher in 1884 was producing the first Saskatoon newspaper. Its three issues each consisted of a single handwritten copy.

Teacher George Horn and his class in front of the stone schoolhouse in 1892. Built on the site where Victoria School now stands, the little stone school was also the center of social activities, including the 1888 New Year's party — which everyone in Saskatoon attended!

The Northwest Mounted Police "barracks" in the late 1880s, a house on Dufferin Avenue. Notice the telephone wire which connected the settlement with the Dominion Telegraph Office at Clarkboro, about twelve miles north of Saskatoon.

Lumber brought in (in 1889) for a bridge built to carry the Qu'Appelle, Long Lake, and Saskatchewan Railway. The line extended as far north as Prince Albert. School children from the west side had to cross this railway bridge until the "Pioneer School," the first school on the west bank, was constructed in 1901.

The first cash commodity shipped from Saskatoon to eastern markets — buffalo bones gathered on the surrounding prairies. The bones were stacked in the shape and size of boxcars at First Avenue, along the railway, where Midtown Plaza now stands.

The west bank settlement viewed from the Nutana side in about 1891. The white line to the right of the railway station is a pile of buffalo bones.

The turntable, a revolving platform used to change direction at the end of the railway line. Muscle power was needed to move locomotives on the turntable in front of the two-bay engine house, located near the water tower on the west side in 1894.

The station, one of the first structures, along with the water tower and engine house, on the west side of the river. Notice the buffalo bones piled behind the station.

The Caswell family's sod house near Clarkboro in 1893, just before it was abandoned. The gentleman in the top hat is a vaudeville comedian passing through Saskatoon on the train.

Waiting for the ferry. In the background is the high wooded Nutana river bank. Given ice, sandbars, a slow current, and a ferry master who also held other, better paying jobs in the settlement, service was irregular!

The original Grace Methodist Church in Nutana, named after Grace Fletcher, a local storekeeper and buffalo-bone buyer.

A view of Saskatoon from the top of the flour mill in 1903. The buildings of Nutana are visible on the horizon. The new railway "roundhouse" and Immigration Hall are seen at right center in the picture.

The Northwest Mounted Police barracks located on First Avenue between Nineteenth and Twentieth streets in 1897. The detachment had moved from the Nutana settlement after the construction of the railway.

Chapter 3
Three Settlements Become a City (1903·1907)

The local economy received a substantial boost with the arrival of the Barr colonists in 1903. Some 1,500 people on their way to the Britannia Colony (now Lloydminster) camped in tents beside the railway while supplies were obtained from local merchants; then the party moved west along the Battleford Trail.

Nutana decided on incorporation as a village in 1903. Its population, like that of Saskatoon, was increasing steadily. In addition, a new subdivision was starting where the Barr colonists' tents had stood. No high-minded principles of community planning were evident here: The lots were small and the streets narrow, and there was minimal public reserve. Saskatoon Town Council protested that this new settlement, without health or building bylaws and without fire protection, constituted a danger. In 1905 the new subdivision was incorporated as a separate village named "Riversdale."

Important developments in Saskatoon included a new flour mill, a couple of banks, and a growing number of real estate firms. A new school district was established, and a four-room brick school built on the west bank, to be named King Edward after the recently crowned king. A small telephone system was installed, a police force inaugurated, and fire-fighting equipment purchased. The roads were graded, and plank sidewalks were constructed along the main streets. More ambitious buildings were rising: the Empire and King Edward hotels, new stores, and new churches. Fine new homes lined the river banks, and the first horseless carriages were startling the local horses.

Not all went well during these years. In two successive springs — 1904 and 1905 — the ice, breaking up and flowing down the swollen river, took virtually the whole railway bridge with it; but new trestles were soon built and the rails re-laid. Rumors that the Canadian Northern Railway would come this way were dashed when it was routed ten miles north, through Warman. A more lasting disappointment came in 1905 when Regina, not Saskatoon, was chosen as capital of the new province of Saskatchewan.

There were health problems also. Some water was being obtained from wells in yards and in the streets where barns and livery stables became pollution hazards. However, most water came from the river into which refuse was dumped. Predictably, there was a series of typhoid epidemics which hit the many railway construction camps especially hard. When fires broke out, there was difficulty in obtaining water to combat them. A hospital was needed, as was a power station. Such facilities cost money, more money than the three settlements could individually either provide or borrow.

Cooperation was the only solution. In the summer of 1905, representatives from Saskatoon, Nutana, and Riversdale met and agreed on amalgamation. The combined population of the settlements was close to 4,500, a figure which allowed application for city status. On July 1, 1906, as one of its earliest actions, the newly formed government of Saskatchewan granted a charter. Saskatoon became a city.

A train carrying Barr colonists arriving at the station in Saskatoon in April, 1903.

Preparing for the journey to the Lloydminster area. During the outfitting period, the colonists provided themselves with many services, including, as the sign says, "shaving and haircuts."

Temporary dwellings of the Barr colonists. A tent and shack city arose on the west side between the Immigration Hall and the railway station.

The Barr colonists getting ready to embark overland to the Britannia Colony, now Lloydminster.

Two future Saskatonians camped in Riversdale, probably in 1904 since the temporary railway bridge, erected after the ice damage that spring, can be seen in the background. The large white building in the left rear is the Immigration Hall.

A group of recently arrived bachelors who had a postcard made of this scene in front of a tent on Avenue H. Maybe they intended to send copies of this one home to their mothers . . .

. . . and to send copies of this one home to their friends!

Empire Day celebrations in 1904. A large crowd assembled at the new King Edward School on Twenty-third Street north of town. City Hall is on this site now.

First Avenue and Twentieth Street, the most important corner in town because the railway station, from which this picture was taken, was located there.

The teller, seemingly well protected at the wicket of the Union Bank of Canada branch at Twenty-first Street and Second Avenue, 1905.

First Avenue in about 1905. The second Windsor Hotel, built only a few years later on the same site, still stands today.

A bachelor residence on Avenue F, the edge of the city in 1906. Most men in Saskatoon at that time either were single or had left their families behind until they established themselves. The man in the doorway, Austin Needham, still lives in Saskatoon.

The "uniform" of Saskatoon businessmen. It appears to have included a hat and a tie, but obviously nobody said anything about style or size! This real estate firm represented a number of land companies including the Temperance Colonization Society, which by that time was no longer concerned about temperance.

A sleighing party on First Avenue. Usually the sleigh would have been used for practical transportation rather than for fun outings.

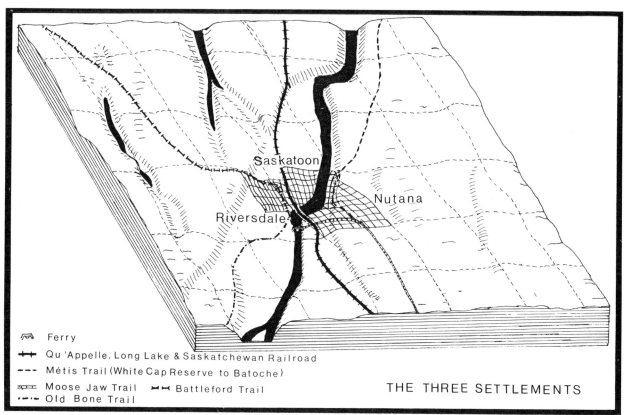

Ferry

Qu'Appelle, Long Lake & Saskatchewan Railroad

Métis Trail (White Cap Reserve to Batoche)

Moose Jaw Trail   Battleford Trail
Old Bone Trail

THE THREE SETTLEMENTS

The three settlements, which were to amalgamate as the city of Saskatoon in 1906.

Commercial travellers stranded in Saskatoon, posed on the bank about where the Broadway Bridge stands today. The railway bridge, shown in the background, went out with the ice in 1904.

The "Long Hill" down to the ferry. When another photograph appeared as a postcard, it was labelled "Lover's Lane, Nutana." The title does not appear appropriate for this narrow, muddy track since it was the busiest roadway in the whole community.

The temporary replacement bridge, which went out with the ice in 1905. The three houses shown at the left on the Nutana side are those that served as hospitals during the Riel Rebellion in 1885. The large one on the extreme left is still standing today at 326 Eleventh Street.

The ferry in operation. It did not have an engine as do river ferries now but depended on the river current to move it across. This picture shows the railway bridge as rebuilt with concrete piers in 1905, to prevent further ice problems in the spring.

The ferry, the vehicle for everything moving between Nutana and Saskatoon. This 1907 picture shows the uncompleted Traffic Bridge (now commonly called the Victoria Bridge) at the left.

A steel girder being lowered into place at the Nutana end of the Traffic Bridge in the summer of 1907.

WALK YOUR HORSES
AUTOMOBILES NOT TO EXCEED
6 MILES PER HOUR

Completion of the Traffic Bridge. The unreliable ferry service was replaced by relatively easy access between the east and west sides.

The construction of the CPR bridge, still standing at the east end of Thirty-third Street. When the Canadian Northern Railway bought the original line which had been leased to the CPR, the CPR built its own track, this bridge, and a station to give access to the city.

Horse-drawn buses waiting at the CPR station to take new arrivals to the various hotels. The busy station handled trains arriving or departing almost one after another all day long.

Saskatonians of all ages, dressed in their best clothes for the opening of the Traffic Bridge on October 6, 1907. Among the features visible on the Nutana side are the "Long Hill," the new two-storey Nutana school, and Grace Methodist Church.

The town of Saskatoon at about the time of amalgamation with Riversdale and Nutana. The King Edward School dominates the town. The Caswells' farm can be seen on the hill directly behind the school.

Chapter 4
The Boom Years (1908 · 1914)

In 1907 Saskatoon was just a large prairie town with only modest prospects for growth. Five years later it was being described as "The Wonder City," "The Chicago of the Prairies," and the "fastest growing city in the British Empire." In 1912 estimates of Saskatoon's population varied from 12,000 (the Dominion census figure) to about 28,000 (the board of trade's figure). Whatever the actual population, the growth was so rapid that predictions of reaching 200,000 in 1930 and 400,000 by 1940 seemed reasonable. Land values were inflating concomitantly. Downtown lots that in 1901 would have fetched only $5 for each twenty-five feet of frontage already were fetching $300 in 1903; by 1912 they were selling for $1,700 per front foot. For real estate agents and for their more astute customers, land investment was indeed a bonanza!

Many factors contributed to this growth. The original Qu'Appelle, Long Lake, and Saskatchewan line was taken over by the Canadian Northern Railway, and after early problems, better services were inaugurated; soon the Grand Trunk Pacific and Canadian Pacific were constructing new lines that made Saskatoon the "Hub City" of the prairies. By 1912, twenty-seven passenger trains were arriving at or leaving the city daily.

Homesteads were still available in Canada but no longer in the United States. This fact, vigorously advertised by the Dominion government and by the railroads, diverted northward the flow of settlers from Europe. An active board of trade, a very vocal Industrial League, and many private entrepreneurs busily advertised the attractions of Saskatoon in terms often wildly transcending reality.

By 1913 forty square miles had been subdivided, with a number of new industrial town sites such as "Factoria," "Mackenzie," and "Swastika Park" advertised for development outside the city limits. Though much of this real estate was being held on speculation, there had been a great deal of building. Large brick and concrete warehouses were interspersed among the wood and tin-clad sheds along the railroad tracks. The wholesale-retail function had greatly expanded. Industries that opened included the John East Ironworks, the Quaker Oats mill, a brewery, and an automobile assembly plant. In the central business district, large commercial blocks echoing the styles of Chicago and Winnipeg had risen: the Ross Block, the Standard Trust Building, the Drinkle buildings, and the Canada Building.

The variety of languages heard and the diverse ethnic apparel visible on the streets, the increasing number of Jewish shops and Chinese restaurants made apparent the changing composition of Saskatoon's population. Fine new churches were rising, testifying to a greater admixture of religious faiths and sects. Though the British tradition remained paramount, as the continuing popularity of cricket and association football made evident, newer sports were becoming a part of city life. During the winter a local hockey team entertained crowds in a covered rink. In the summers a semiprofessional baseball team, composed largely of American imports, played on the new Cairns Field. Touring companies, the "flickers," and annual exhibitions added to the variety of entertainment, and always there were the pool halls and bars.

New elementary schools were opened on the fringes of the expanding city, plus a collegiate located at the south end of the Traffic Bridge on the Nutana hill. A Catholic separate school system was organized in 1913, operating in a church basement until permanent quarters could be constructed. The YMCA and YWCA both opened on downtown sites; and a public library was located in the basement of the Oddfellows' Hall.

Saskatonians were proud when their city was chosen in 1909 as the site for the provincial university. The campus, located on the high eastern bank of the river, became a hub of activity as greystone buildings in "collegiate-gothic" style were constructed about an oval promenade soon to be known as "the bowl." The university rapidly became a major influence, not only on the cultural life of the city but also on its character.

City council, at first reluctant to go into debt to provide badly needed services and utilities, was soon caught up by the optimism of the times. Between 1909 and 1913 major capital works projects undertaken included sewer and water systems, expanded electrical services, paving of the streets, a street railway system, and an underpass under the railway in the downtown area. The King Edward School building was acquired in 1910 to serve as a new City Hall, a replacement school being built in City Park to the north. In 1912, a city commissioner was hired, and the ward system was inaugurated to improve administration of civic affairs. Council was in process of adding $2 million more to its $8 million debt when the economy of western Canada, and indeed of much of the western world, suddenly slumped. The boom was over.

Billy Silverwood — local livery stable owner, horse raiser, and entrepreneur who sold bottled spring water during the years of typhoid epidemics. The picture was taken on Twentieth Street between First and Second avenues. Silverwood went bankrupt in 1913 and was unable to move into his new orange-brick home at Queen Street and Eighth Avenue.

The livery stable which stood on First Avenue between Twenty-first and Twenty-second streets. The man holding the horse on the extreme right is Dr. Girling, a veterinarian who died in the Great War. To his right is George Potter, who owned the business when this picture was taken in 1908.

Canadian Northern Railway train entering downtown Saskatoon over the original railway bridge in 1908. By the end of that year, the city was served by three railway companies — Canadian Northern Railway, Canadian Pacific Railway, and Grand Trunk Pacific Railway Company.

The effects of the floods of 1908 on the flats on Saskatchewan Crescent West.

The midway of the fair in 1909. Traces of this race track may still be seen at the site in City Park (now Kinsmen Park).

The S. S. *City of Medicine Hat*, the last large paddle steamer on the South Saskatchewan. The ship hit the Traffic Bridge during the 1908 high water . . .

"Broken-Backed". (Wreck of the "City of Medicine Hat." Saskatoon, June 17, 1908.) photo by City Studio.

. . . and sank. As one local photographer captioned a postcard, it was "the greatest marine disaster in the history of Saskatoon!"

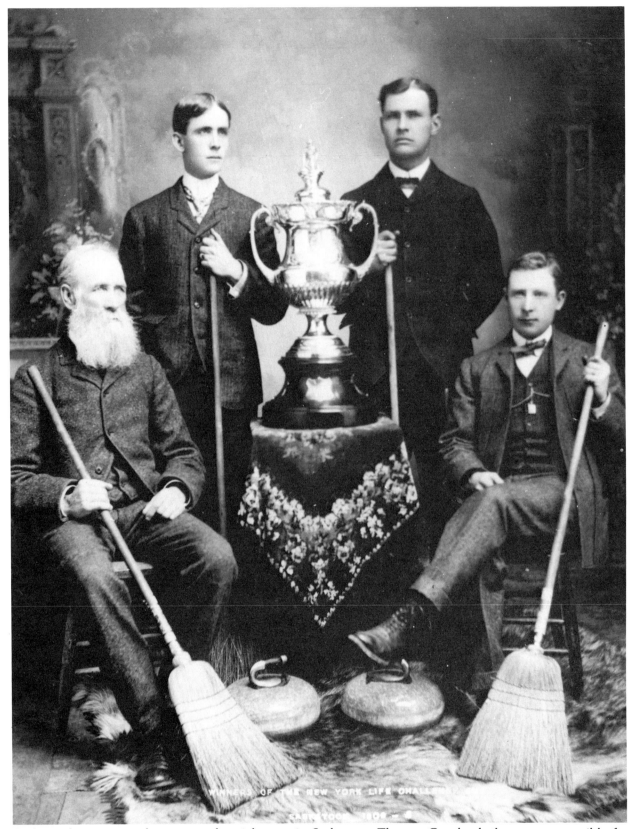

Curling, always a popular sport and social event in Saskatoon. Thomas Copeland, the man responsible for planning the broad streets downtown, is on the left.

Filling a hot-air balloon at the fairgrounds in 1908. It was another four years before an airplane was seen in Saskatoon; in the meantime, crowds thrilled to the stately ascent of a balloon.

Second Avenue, still not paved in 1910 although it had quickly built up with two- and three-storey brick buildings.

John East Ironworks, one of the first manufacturing businesses in Saskatoon.

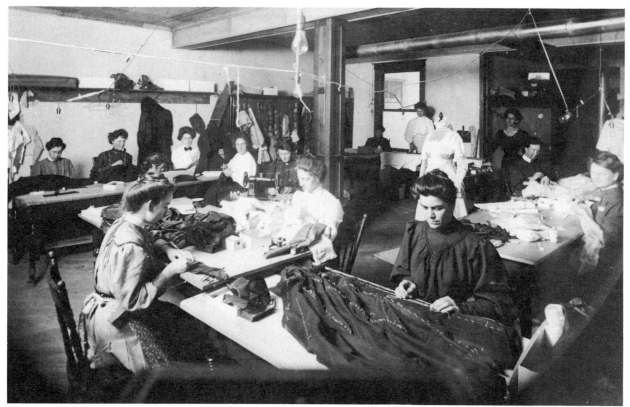

The dressmaking department of the J. F. Cairns Store. Clothing was not available "off the rack" at the beginning of the century as it is today.

Sutherland, the development which grew up across Central Avenue from the CPR yards. Founded in 1907, it was a typical small railway town with cramped streets and closely spaced lots.

Sutherland School towering above the fields — almost an island in the midst of a good crop.

The National Trust Block during fair week, 1910. Today the building is occupied by Folk's Furs and, without the board sidewalks, dirt streets, and horse-drawn bus, looks quite different.

Sir Wilfrid Laurier officiating at the ceremonies when construction of the College (Administration) Building of the new university was begun in 1910.

Saskatoon's Sons of England football team, one of the best soccer teams in the province.

A steam-powered machine digging trenches for sewer lines.

Third Avenue, the scene of frantic activity. Almost all the buildings between Twentieth and Twenty-second streets were constructed at the same time.

Twenty-first Street seen from both directions in 1912. The Canada Building, under construction at the time, may be seen in the upper picture. In the lower picture a solitary horse-drawn wagon and a steamroller share the streets with the motor cars.

A circus parade turning the corner of First Avenue and Twentieth Street. The photographer was standing on the steps of the pedestrian bridge over the railway yards.

Initial work on the Municipal Street Railway, which did not actually begin running until 1913. Although planned, a hydroelectric dam was not built in the river.

The window display of the Streatham Newsagency. What is now the Saskatoon Book Store was pretty forward in trying to snare customers from among those of British origin.

Mayor James Clinkskill chatting with the governor general, His Royal Highness the duke of Connaught, at ceremonies in City Park during the viceregal visit in 1912. The new King Edward School is visible in the background.

Second Avenue in 1913 or 1914, looking very metropolitan with pavement, streetcars, a policeman in a "bobby" type helmet, and businessmen in abundance.

Rail accident in March, 1912. The last cars of a Canadian Northern train jumped the track as they passed out of the railway yards. Dragged onto the bridge, they knocked out one span. The sleeping car *Kipling* fell onto the ice, injuring thirteen people. The wreckage was later removed by a steam crane.

"Stand-up" bars for men only, once common in hotels. This one was the Flanagan (later the Senator) Hotel bar in September, 1912.

Absalom Rice's confectionery store on Broadway Avenue. Denied entrance to the "men-only" bars, women used the corner cafe and confectionery as a gathering place.

One of the original twelve streetcars, as seen in later years. These "puddle jumpers" were bought secondhand in St. Louis, Missouri. Because their wheels were in the center, they could be rocked by rambunctious passengers (such as university students) standing in the ends of the cars.

The 600 block of Broadway North (University Drive), lined with substantial houses where there had been only empty prairie shortly before.

A girls' physical education class in bloomers on the lawn of the Collegiate. The Indian clubs in their hands were flourished in synchronized patterns to improve coordination.

July 4, 1913. Saskatonians of American origin paraded on Twenty-first Street, at the time a dirt street with board sidewalks. All the buildings shown, except the bank on the right, are still standing today.

A view of downtown, Nutana, and the university, probably taken from the top of the new Canada Building. Numerous buildings were constructed in a few short years.

Another photograph from the top of the Canada Building. Among the new buildings shown are the Queen's Hotel, the Hoeschen-Wentzler Brewery (now Labatts), Arctic Ice, the waterworks, and the power plant.

The Victoria or Marble Palace Barber Shop, next to the Victoria Theatre on Second Avenue in 1913. Notice the cuspidors on the floor, the shoeshine stand, and the sign at the foot of the stairs advertising baths.

The first mayor of the city of Saskatoon, James Clinkskill, seen here in the study of his home on Nineteenth Street.

The Crescent Rink, where the famous Cook brothers played. The home of the Saskatoon Sheik and Crescent hockey teams, it was replaced in 1937 by the Arena.

City Hospital, one of the new hospitals built to accommodate the city's growing population. Construction was spurred by the typhoid epidemics before the sewer and water lines were installed.

Chapter 5
Years of the Great War (1914·1918)

By early 1914 Saskatoon was deep in recession. Tightening money and political unrest in Europe had reduced the flow of capital and immigrants to the prairies. Businesses began to close their doors and construction stopped. Real estate values plummeted and many speculators sold their holdings cheaply. Frequently those that hung on had to forfeit their property later in lieu of unpaid taxes. The city government cut back sharply, leaving some partially developed areas unserviced; even so, the remaining citizens found themselves saddled with a large civic debt. The consequence was a scattered cityscape, with many empty lots and uncompleted buildings.

When Britain declared war on Germany in August, 1914, the men of the Saskatoon region quickly responded to the call to arms. Within two weeks the first volunteers left to join eastern regiments. Soon after, the 105th Regiment *Fusiliers* (Saskatoon), which became part of the 11th Battalion Canadian Expeditionary Force, and the 29th Light Horse were moved to eastern military camps for further training and then shipped overseas. A further 1,600 men were raised for the 65th Battalion and a full battalion joined the 96th Highlanders. Three platoons were raised from the university, joining the 196th Western Universities Battalion, and a number of men joined the Royal Flying Corps and the Royal Canadian Navy. In all, more than 10,000 men from the Saskatoon region served in the armed forces.

Local merchants and organizations supported the war effort by collecting funds, financing the purchase of military equipment, and preparing parcels to be sent to the troops overseas. Over half a million dollars' worth of Victory Bonds were purchased in Saskatoon. The new YMCA was transformed into a military convalescent hospital, and an armory was constructed at the end of the Traffic Bridge.

The renewed demand for beef and grain stabilized the economy, but rationing of strategic materials hampered any new construction in the city. There were only three major building projects during this period: a five-storey extension to the Eaton's warehouse on Avenue D, a large new government elevator on the city's western fringe, and a second traffic bridge at Twenty-fifth Street, completed by the provincial government after the original contractors went bankrupt.

The new bridge was urgently needed, for automobile and truck traffic was increasing greatly. With the men away at war, women drivers were becoming a common sight. Indeed, women were working in many jobs hitherto closed to them; they were even to be found as bank tellers and barbers! It was because of their growing political influence that prohibiton was enforced in Saskatoon after 1914, closing the bars and, at the end of 1916, government liquor stores too. However, the drinkers did not have to travel far. Importation of liquor was a federal matter, and until April of 1918, purchases could still be made from import shops and drugstores.

Though the battles were being fought many thousand miles away, the posters on the walls, the military parades, the newspaper headlines of victories or defeats, and the disheartening casualty lists made the war a part of everyday life in Saskatoon. When the Armistice was announced just after midnight on November 11, 1918, there was great jubilation. The *Phoenix* had an extra edition on the streets three minutes after official receipt of the news. Bonfires and parades went on into the early morning.

Celebration was tempered, however, by the epidemic of Spanish influenza then sweeping the city, the sorry condition of so many returning soldiers, and the memory of so many who would never return.

The Canadian Government Elevator, completed in 1915, located on the west side of the city where the three railways converged. It enabled the cleaning and storage of large quantities of grain in the interior of the country, ready for export.

Early days on the new campus. Saskatchewan Hall, the women's residence, had been completed in 1913. The open spaces between the scattered buildings were put to good use.

The 2nd Contingent of the 105th *Fusiliers* casually posed for a group photo opposite the old Armories on Fourth Avenue at Spadina Crescent. They received their basic training there before being moved east for further training and then being shipped overseas.

A practical course in "School Gardening" for teachers, offered as a credit summer class by the College of Agriculture in 1914. The new lumber mill visible in the right background in the City Park district across the river burned down in 1980.

Three local volunteers, members of one of the three platoons from the University of Saskatchewan which were part of the 196th Western University Battalion. Two, J. E. Einarson and Allan Macmillan, were killed in action. The third (top left), John G. Diefenbaker, returned to become a prominent Saskatchewan lawyer and later prime minister of Canada.

Friends, neighbors, and relatives cheering local recruits marching down into the Twenty-third Street subway to the CPR station, bound for eastern military camps.

The 2nd Contingent turning the corner at Twenty-first Street and First Avenue en route to the Canadian Northern Railway yards, where they boarded trains for the east.

Saskatoon police vehicles parked behind City Hall.

Experimental model, 1918. Professor R. D. McLaurin of the chemistry department of the university tested a motor powered by gases obtained from decaying straw — a commodity readily available in the region.

The Twenty-fifth Street Bridge under construction in the summer of 1916.

Sergeant Hugh Cairns, member of a prominent Saskatoon family, posthumously awarded the Victoria Cross for bravery during the advance before Valenciennes in November, 1918.

The YMCA on Spadina Crescent, used as a temporary convalescent hospital in Saskatoon during the Great War.

The Saskatoon Junior Symphony Orchestra under the direction of Mr. Max Tomczak, its conductor from 1917 to 1920.

The Victoria Theatre on Second Avenue (present location of the Odeon Theatre), one of the first motion picture palaces in Saskatoon. It incorporated the Marble Palace Barber Shop, seen on an earlier page.

Typical advertisements of Saskatoon businesses during the war years.

Chapter 6
Prosperity Regained
(1919 • 1929)

The transition from war to peacetime was not an easy one. Throughout the western world this was a period of economic and political turmoil. Veterans returning to Saskatoon were aided in their search for housing and jobs by various local organizations, but prosperity was not swiftly regained. The postwar slump in agricultural prices caused a recession in local industry and business, and there was a considerable delay before goods and construction materials again became freely available. There was both political and labor unrest, though these were less serious here than in some other Canadian cities.

Those who had fallen in the Great War were commemorated by plaques and other memorials in and on city buildings. A cenotaph which became the focus for Remembrance Day services, military parades, and civic celebrations in the ensuing decades was erected on Twenty-first Street.

Yet, slowly but surely, the wartime shadows passed. By the mid-twenties the markets had recovered and prospects were improving. Though the rapid expansion of the boom period found no postwar parallel, there was a renewed flow of immigrants to the region, and the last sections of arable land were brought under cultivation.

During the 1920s Ukrainians and other immigrants were under increasing pressure to assimilate. The Ukrainians in particular reacted by closing ranks. The Mohyla Institute had opened in 1916; new churches and associations helped strengthen their sense of pride and identity during the decades that followed.

Some newcomers found employment in Saskatoon's expanding industries and businesses. The Massey-Harris and Rumely farm implement companies constructed large warehouses in the industrial area between the railways; Robin Hood Flour bought the old Factoria mill north of the city and began a new mill of its own on Thirty-third Street; and the Union Stockyard opened, west on Eleventh Street. The two major merchandising firms, Eaton's and the Hudson's Bay Company, moved to larger quarters, buying the former MacMillan Department Store and J. F. Cairns Store respectively, and a number of new businesses opened. Under such stimulus building permits rose to $6 million by 1929, and the population of Saskatoon climbed to over 40,000.

The facilities of the city were greatly upgraded. New buildings on the university campus, a Normal School and several primary and secondary schools, a new public library, and a police station were erected. A new Federal Building including an enlarged post office was started; a sanatorium was constructed and a major addition was built to City Hospital.

With technological advances and increasing incomes, Saskatonians were finding new entertainments and diversions. The Saskatoon Aero Club at the Air Harbour to the northwest of the city claimed to be the largest in the province. Three radio stations went on the air, making people more aware than ever before of the larger world about them and the variety of consumer goods to be had. The city's two newspapers amalgamated as the *Star-Phoenix*. Movies and live entertainment were available in the sumptuous surroundings of the new Capitol Theatre. Sport continued to be popular, with semiprofessional baseball and hockey packing in the fans and with golf, horse riding, and auto touring for the more affluent. Ethel Catherwood, the local girl who won a gold medal at the 1928 Olympics, was the pride of the city.

Temperance remained a stormy topic. The "ban-the-bar" organizations seemed to have won for a while. However, though the province was nominally "dry" except for a brief "wet" period after the war, it was never so in fact; "medicinal stimulants," stockpiled supplies, home brew, and bootleggers kept the thirsty supplied. In 1924, after a "Great Wet Rally" attracted 1,500 people in Saskatoon, there came partial repeal and the reopening of government liquor stores. A second focus for controversy was the ward system for civic elections, repealed in 1920.

Despite their easier access to world news, Saskatonians remained immersed in these questions and in other regional matters such as grain prices and freight rates. Like Canadians generally they were preoccupied with getting the most out of life, be they university students concerned with campus fads and antics, housewives enjoying new domestic conveniences, or men taking pride in their new cars. The youth of the twenties had come to expect a comfortable living and continued prosperity. They were in no way prepared for the hardships to come.

Downtown Saskatoon in the early 1920s. "Chinatown" was concentrated in old dwellings and business places on Nineteenth Street, at the end of Second Avenue. At the end of the decade, this area was cleared to provide a central site for the Technical School, a new Legion building, and later the Arena. The center of the Chinese community then shifted to the "west side."

Hyslop. McClelland. Campbell

McClelland-Aircraft
1921

McClelland Aviation, situated west of St. Paul's Hospital. The scene was busier than usual in August, 1920, when U.S. Army Airforce planes, flying from Washington D.C. to Alaska, stopped to refuel in Saskatoon. McClelland and his fellow pilots offered flying lessons and served the central Saskatchewan area, carrying passengers for business and pleasure.

Laying the cornerstone of the provincial Normal School, a training center for teachers on Avenue A, in 1921. It was officially opened in 1923. Another provincial institution, the sanatorium, was erected in Saskatoon in 1925 for the treatment of tuberculosis, which had reached epidemic proportions after the war.

Keng Wah Aviation, established north of the city on the site of the present airport in 1919. The company trained young Nationalist Chinese to fly and maintain their Curtiss Jenny JN-4 aircraft. Later the location became the base for a local flying club. In 1928 city council purchased the site to provide a suitable airport, which was called the Air Harbour.

Saskatoon's first radio station, CFQC. It went on the air on July 18, 1923, broadcasting from this small building which served as both studio and transmitter. It was located at 1323 Osler Street, just south of the university campus. Two years later its broadcast times had to be coordinated with that of two other small stations because they were all on the same frequency.

The original microphone and transmitter. The station sometimes had to be shut down for a minute or two in order to loosen the carbon in the microphone.

The Saskatoon Crescents hockey team, Western Canadian Junior Champions in 1921, posed in front of the Crescent Rink. The senior team played in the Western Canada Professional League — the fastest league in the world until the formation of the NHL.

The Chemistry Building, in which the established "collegiate gothic" style was maintained. It was erected on the north side of "the bowl" in 1924. Containing large laboratories and a tiered lecture theatre, it was one of the most up-to-date educational facilities in the country. The Physics Building, just behind it, had been completed three years earlier.

City officials greeting Ethel Catherwood on her return from the 1928 Olympics in Amsterdam, where she had won a gold medal with a record high jump of 5 feet 3 inches. A graduate of Bedford Road Collegiate, she had trained under Joe Griffiths at the university in Saskatoon.

The inevitable result of an increased number of automobiles on the streets in the 1920s. An increased number of collisions occurred, such as this one at Main and Lorne between a train and two "liveries" taking people to and from the exhibition in July, 1928. Four lives were lost in the accident. That intersection is now part of the approach to the Idylwyld Bridge.

Governor General Baron Byng of Vimy narrowly missing a long putt on the last hole at the Saskatoon Golf and Country Club during a viceregal visit to Saskatoon in 1922. Mayor McConnell holds the pin while an aide-de-camp and local citizens look on. This golf club was originally established in City Park (Kinsmen Park) in 1907 and then moved to a site on the exhibition grounds across Lorne Avenue from the Grand Trunk Pacific Railway roundhouse and yards. The young caddy, Bill Kinnear, was to become a respected pediatrician and prominent citizen of Saskatoon.

The fiery destruction of the Drinkle No. 1 Building in 1925. Before the First World War, the University of Saskatchewan held classes in this building. Rebuilt and renamed the MacMillan Building, it now stands at the corner of Second Avenue and Twenty-first Street.

Twenty-first Street, following a snowstorm which brought the city to a standstill in the middle of March, 1927.

A gowned procession on the way to Convocation Hall on the campus for the 1928 graduation ceremony. Enrolments at the university had risen sharply after World War I, reaching 1,460 by the end of the twenties.

The Memorial Gates, dedicated in 1928 — the result of years of effort by university students to honor former colleagues who had been killed in the Great War. The little stone schoolhouse had been moved from its original site at Victoria and Broadway by W. P. Bate, the first secretary-treasurer of School District No. 13, with support from the I.O.D.E. and reconstructed on the campus in 1911.

The operators at the telegraph office, located on Second Avenue and Twenty-second Street, pausing to pose for a picture in 1923. Most of the information of current business and economic concern sent to or from Saskatoon passed through this office.

The interior of the public library, constructed on the corner of Third Avenue and Twenty-third Street in 1928. Since it was next to the No. 1 Fire Hall and directly opposite City Hall, the beginning of a civic square was in the making. A new police station was built across the street from the fire hall the following year.

The Saskatoon Yacht Club in Victoria Park, just up river from the Civic Swimming Pool and the water works. Club activities provided relaxation for members on warm summer days.

A power shovel excavating the site of the new Eaton's department store at Third Avenue and Twenty-first Street in 1929. The Great War Veterans Association building, which had housed the public library, had formerly occupied this site.

The Civic Swimming Pool (now Riversdale Pool), completed in 1926 — a mecca for many local residents on hot summer afternoons. With its convenient change rooms and fountain, the new pool was a great improvement over its predecessor. The former swimming hole, adjacent to the Yacht Club dock, had been formed by a floating log boom in the river.

The Capitol Theatre, constructed on Second Avenue in 1929, one of the large luxurious theatres built in major centers across the country to usher in "talking" films. It also served the city as an auditorium and concert hall for many years.

The elaborate interior of the Capitol, a mirror of the fantasies displayed on the screen. One entered along a long, elegantly decorated corridor which opened into the 1,200-seat theatre decorated with Spanish-styled make-believe houses overlooking castle walks. In the domed roof were visible clouds drifting across a twinkling, star-lit sky, all projected by an automatically operated machine called a *Brenograph*.

Loading the wares of The Saskatoon Brewing Co. Limited. The production of beer at the local brewery, like the sale of alcoholic beverages generally, varied with the shift in provincial and local plebiscites from "wet" to "dry" and back again during the 1920s.

One of the first Ukrainian dance schools in North America, established by Vasif Avramenko in Saskatoon in 1927.

Model T runabout. The increasing numbers of automobiles on the streets of Saskatoon were a reflection of the prosperity of the mid to late twenties. Note the chains on the rear wheels.

Ed's Service Station in 1924. The business then occupied the original police and fire station on Twenty-first Street and Third Avenue. The British Columbia-based Gregory Tire and Rubber Co. Ltd. went bankrupt later that same year.

Ice on the banks of the South Saskatchewan River, spring, 1928. The annual ice breakup posed a risk of flooding and damage to bridges.

Chapter 7
=Dust and Depression=
(1929 • 1939)

The impact of the stock market crash of 1929 and the depression that ensued was less immediate in Saskatoon than in many other Canadian cities. Crop yields and prices had been good that year, and a number of major construction projects were already under way, serving to buoy up the economy into the following year. The largest of these projects was a Canadian National luxury hotel being built on the river bank to face the station down the length of Twenty-first Street, and the last was the School for the Deaf, begun in June, 1930. Construction of the hotel was delayed by labor strife as the depression deepened, but when the Bessborough was at last finished in 1935, it became the dominant feature of the riverside and the trademark of the city.

Having struck late, the depression deepened quickly. By early 1931 many families were on relief, dependent on the indulgence of charitable organizations and on a relief board administered by the city with the province providing two thirds of its expenses. The federal government sponsored a program of relief works which included, during 1931, the construction of a subway or underpass under the railway at Nineteenth Street, a system of storm sewers, and a City Hospital nurses' residence. Nevertheless, by September, 1931, the number of families on relief had risen to 1,007.

In the ensuing years, drought, wind, grasshoppers, and falling prices combined to cripple the prairie farm community. During 1932 work on the Broadway Bridge gave jobs to many, but later "make work" projects were smaller — tree planting and park development along the river and construction of the weir were examples. By 1934 the civic relief system had collapsed, and the relief appeal board that had replaced it strove desperately to cope with a progressively worsening situation. The Saskatoon Board of Trade mounted a major campaign, especially at the annual exhibitions, to attract industry to the city. The Hiway Refinery close to the stockyards and several processing plants were opened or enlarged. A regional bus service was established, and the expanded Air Harbour became a stopping point on the new national air route.

Despite these efforts, depression and drought maintained their stubborn hold on the region. In the city, unemployment continued to increase. Many individuals and some whole families packed up and left. Destitute men passing through the city, many "riding the rods" of freight trains, were billeted and fed at the Exhibition Grounds; sometimes as many as 500 were encamped there. Vagabonds were picked up and sent to work building the army camp near Dundurn.

Dust clouds, "Bennett buggies," and closed businesses became common sights. Jam pail lunch boxes, homemade furniture, and secondhand clothing became the way of life for many. The few dwellings constructed in the thirties were small and unserviced. In order to cut housing costs, families often doubled up, occupying basements or back yard garages. Many young people postponed or abandoned plans to attend secondary school or university in order to help support their families and themselves. Movies, radios, and booze provided, for young and old alike, the only diversions from day-to-day hardships.

Yet in spite of their difficulties, Saskatonians somehow contrived to keep up their spirits and to believe that things must be better "next year." A "pay-your-taxes" campaign by the board of trade in 1935 was surprisingly successful. The Arena rink, built through the initiative of local service clubs on voluntary contributions and opened in 1937, served as an expression of local confidence.

That confidence seemed unrequited by the crop failures and blighted hopes of that summer of 1938, when twenty percent of the population were on relief at a cost to the city of almost $200,000. Yet the tide was turning. Prices were rising again; industrial activity was quickening; and at last the economy was showing signs of growth.

When the new king and queen visited the city in June, 1939, Saskatonians turned out in their finest array to express their loyalty. It was to be only months before this loyalty was tested, when war once again broke out in Europe.

Second Avenue in 1930. The crowds were just breaking up after the passing of the Travellers' Day Parade, a highlight of exhibition week in Saskatoon for many years.

A view of Saskatoon and area from the southwest in 1930. The sanatorium (lower center) was well outside the city at that time. Development had remained quite scattered since the collapse of the boom in 1913.

Local dignitaries watching the pilot, D. R. McLaren, fuel his Fokker at the airport after delivering the first bags of airmail in Saskatoon on the national route established in March, 1930. With the inauguration of airmail service, the city made some improvements to the runways and provided electrical services to enable night flying.

The Bessborough Hotel, named after the earl of Bessborough, the governor general of Canada who officiated at its opening in 1935. This was to be one of the most attractive of the chain of CNR hotels erected in major centers across Canada between the wars.

Dust storms — all too common during the droughts that characterized much of the thirties.

Original decor of the reception area of the Bessborough Hotel. The size and range of facilities that the "Bess" offered made it "the convention center of the province" for many years.

The Nineteenth Street underpass, constructed under the CNR tracks in 1931 as a government relief project. It improved access to the city center from the west side.

The Broadway Bridge, a government relief project designed by C. J. Mackenzie of the College of Engineering at the university and constructed by local labor in 1932. The old Crescent Rink (right background) was torn down to provide access to the new bridge. Streetcars were rerouted from the Traffic Bridge and over the new bridge in 1933.

A "Bennett buggy" on the university campus in 1935. Many cars were adapted to alternate forms of "horse power" when gasoline became too expensive.

A common sight during the thirties. Many left the prairie region during the Great Depression. This destitute Saskatoon blacksmith and family packed their meager belongings and migrated to northern Alberta in search of employment.

One of the first hockey games in the Arena — an exhibition match between the New York Rangers and New York Americans on October 30, 1937. The Arena was described at the time as the finest artificial ice facility in western Canada.

Norm Robson and partner, Margaret Wheelock, practicing on an outdoor rink behind Thornton School for the 1936 Ice Follies. The event was held in the Exhibition Stadium because the new arena had not been completed.

The Hiway Refinery at its Eleventh Street West site. The company started production in 1932, using crude oil hauled from wells in western Saskatchewan. It provided a range of petroleum products to the central area of the province.

Spectators viewing the Travellers' Day Parade as it crossed the Broadway Bridge in 1937. The Bessborough Hotel now dominated the skyline of Saskatoon.

Farm girls at the University of Saskatchewan in 1935. The university offered more than academic programs to residents of the province during the Dirty Thirties.

The ladies' wear department in Adilman's Department Store on Twentieth Street and Avenue B in 1939. As economic conditions improved, business increased.

A portent of better times to come. The sale of new vehicles picked up during the late thirties as employment and wages and the willingness of banks to lend money improved once again.

Construction of a weir, under the auspices of the federal Prairie Farm Rehabilitation Authority, in 1939. The dam was designed to maintain an adequate water level for the city water plant on Avenue H.

The water tower adjacent to No. 3 Fire Hall on the corner of Eleventh Street and Broadway Avenue which supplied the Nutana side of the city. It was one of the three towers constructed during the boom era to provide fire protection and running water for businesses and homes. The other two water towers were located on the west side, in the Caswell Hill and Pleasant Hill areas.

A "human flag," composed of 700 students, and thousands of residents of Saskatoon and region awaiting the arrival of King George VI and Queen Elizabeth at the CNR yards on June 3, 1939.

Saskatoon industries proudly displaying their products for the royal cavalcade passing through the warehouse area.

Chapter 8
=The Second World War= and Its Aftermath (1939·1949)

In September, 1939, following the British declaration of war with Germany, Canada declared war. For a second time, the young men of the Saskatoon region quickly responded to the call to arms. The Saskatoon Light Infantry, successor to the earlier 105th Regiment *Fusiliers*, was mobilized immediately; two months later they were bound for Britain as part of the Canadian 1st Division. Other men and women joined various units of the army, the navy, the air force, the merchant navy, and the auxiliary services. The Exhibition Grounds and a number of warehouses in the city were requisitioned by the federal government, since the existing armories could not accommodate the large numbers enlisting. Recruits to the Saskatoon naval division trained in a downtown service station until 1944, when a new building for HMCS Unicorn was completed.

The municipal airport was taken over by the RCAF to become a flight training school under the British Commonwealth Air Training Plan; many airmen from Australia, New Zealand, and other parts of the British Empire were brought to the city for initial training. New hangars and barracks were hastily constructed, and in 1942 a squadron of the RCAF Women's Division was stationed there to serve as auxiliary staff. Facilities for radio and electronics training were provided at the Technical Collegiate and at the univeristy.

In all, some 7,000 military personnel were stationed in Saskatoon at one time or another during the war. The variety of uniforms to be seen and of accents to be heard in the streets gave a cosmopolitan air to the city. Saskatonians made these strangers welcome. Local businesses and service clubs provided recreation centers; special library privileges were provided for them; and they were welcomed into many homes.

Local industry was soon operating at capacity as wartime demands for agricultural products rose. Intercontinental Pork Packers was set up by Fred Mendel in 1940 and soon was processing 4,000 hogs a week. Cooperative Livestock Producers enlarged its plant, and some smaller companies began operation also. As the population swelled to over 43,000,

housing again became a problem, for a shortage of construction materials precluded the building of new homes. Labor was in short supply. Women filled many jobs formerly held by men, and at harvest time businessmen, office workers, and students helped bring in the crops.

As the war progressed, luxury goods became scarce, restaurants closed one day each week, and strategic materials were rationed. In general, Saskatonians responded well to this regime of austerity, observing the many new regulations and practising emergency civil defense procedures, including blackouts. Newspaper and radio reports were anxiously followed for news of the servicemen involved overseas in such events as the Battle of Britain, the Battle of the Atlantic, the Spitzbergen expedition, the Dieppe landing, the Battle of Monte Cassino, and the Normandy landings. Victories were savored; the growing lists of casualties were dreaded. Fund-raising efforts to provide food and equipment for the troops were strongly supported, and purchases of Victory Bonds often exceeded the campaign objectives.

Relief and jubilation swept the city when news came that the war was over. The returning troops were welcomed, not just by wives, sweethearts, and families, but by the whole community; yet there was mourning also, for those who had died.

Although the emphasis was on returning to peacetime conditions, a military dimension was retained in Saskatoon. In the late 1940s the airport, enlarged to serve regular Trans-Canada Air Lines flights, was designated as the headquarters of 406 Squadron RCAF. The 2nd Battalion North Saskatchewan Regiment was maintained as a permanent unit, housed in new armories on Idylwyld Drive, while the navy continued recruiting and reserve training through HMCS Unicorn.

However, most of the former servicemen and servicewomen returned to civilian life. All three levels of government strove to aid them. Despite a continuing shortage of materials, 300 new dwellings were built with federal aid under the Wartime Housing Act on land supplied by the city. The new residences fell far short of needs, however, for the population had risen to over 50,000. Univeristy registration had more than doubled, with many veterans entering classes under special regulations. Former hangars and H-huts were adapted, not only as classrooms and laboratories but also as lodging for the veterans and their families.

Yet this was an era of optimism. Prices were high; profit margins were secure; harvests in general were good; and jobs were available. The sad times of the Dirty Thirties were firmly behind and the future looked rosy.

The new CNR station, erected in 1939 on the site of the old one. It handled increasing traffic as the economy improved and the Second World War ensued. The cenotaph, dedicated in 1929, was located at the focus of the business area, Second Avenue and Twenty-first Street.

The 1st Battalion of the Saskatoon Light Infantry, commanded by Colonel Potts, on a march along Second Avenue in November, 1939. A month later they entrained for Halifax and then sailed overseas.

The 21st Field Regiment, formed from an existing militia unit in 1939. The group received artillery training at the Exhibition Stadium before being moved east in 1940. The stadium was used as a military training center throughout the war, especially in cold months.

A summertime parade of the ship's company of HMCS Unicorn. The guard, with fixed bayonets, is entering the Nineteenth Street subway. After initial training, most of these men departed for active duty. Prairie boys made some of the best sailors!

City council meeting in the chamber of the old City Hall in 1941. The accommodation of large numbers of servicemen, as well as civilians coming to Saskatoon, was one of the problems with which they had to contend.

The living room of the Gibson home at 308 Lansdowne Avenue in the early war years. The console radio brought anxious listeners hourly updates on action in Europe, as well as episodes of "The Shadow," the humor of the "Happy Gang," and local programs.

The Saskatoon airport, adopted as a British Commonwealth Air Training Plan base in 1940. Numerous additions were made including hangars, barracks, and a radar-equipped observation tower at the main terminal.

Members of the first Women's Division RCAF, based in Saskatoon. Assistant Senior Officer Marion Graham (the driver) was being taken to the downtown clubrooms provided by the Lions in the old telegraph office on Second Avenue for a "send off" party after receiving a new posting in 1942.

Air Training Plan recruits on parade beside the hangar behind the Normal School on Avenue A. The H-huts of the No. 7 Initial Training School are visible in the left background; later this was the site of Kelsey Technical Institute.

The purchase of Victory Bonds, one method by which local residents contributed to the war effort. It is estimated that Saskatonians invested more than $20 million in fund drives, food, and equipment sent overseas during World War II.

A Boy Scout leader making the draw in a Victory Bond lottery at the 1944 exhibition. The Boy Scout movement was very active in Saskatoon during the 1930s and '40s. Scouts acted as ushers at public events and helped with community cleanup campaigns. During the thirties they operated a "fix-it" toy store before Christmas.

October 3, 1945. The Saskatoon Light Infantry were met by a Colour Party when they detrained at the Exhibition Grounds before proceeding to the main station for their official reception. It had been almost six years since the unit had gone abroad.

The Saskatoon Light Infantry pipe band leading a parade of curlers down Twenty-first Street from the Bessborough to the Arena for the Brier Playdowns held in Saskatoon in 1946. Saskatchewan was represented by the D. Henderson rink of the Nutana Club.

No, not an attack on Saskatoon! The scene is "Operation Hub," a tri-service exercise of local reserve units in September, 1948. While the naval reserve carried the militia across the river to a landing on the west side, explosives detonated in the river simulated bombing as Mitchells of the 406th Squadron passed overhead, dropping smoke bombs. The exercise was declared a success. The only "casualties" were the female spectators' nylons, which were destroyed by corrosive agents in the smoke screen.

July 1 baseball tournament. The event, held in 1949 at the old Cairns Field next to the CPR yards on Avenue A and Twenty-fifth Street, drew many spectators. Constructed by a local merchant in 1913, the field had been the scene of many sports days and field meets through the years.

Distinctive "wartime" houses, built for servicemen and their families. The city provided sites, such as the Montgomery Place subdivision, for construction with federal funds. The program was continued after the war to accommodate veterans.

Luxury items such as nylons attracting crowds of local shoppers in the late forties.

Twentieth Street, viewed from the top of the pedestrian railway overpass at Avenue A in the 1940s. It remained a secondary business street, cut off from downtown by the CNR yards, just as Broadway Avenue in Nutana was cut off by the river.

At the end of the forties, the "Three Sisters" and adjacent foundations which had never been built upon. All were products of the pre-World War I boom and had remained isolated on the outskirts of the city at York Avenue and Taylor Street. Two of the houses are still standing today; the third was demolished to make room for a new fire station.

Downtown Saskatoon in 1948, viewed from the north. The amount of open space is striking. Note the formal park behind City Hall and the number of private homes in the area next to the river.

Chapter 9
The Flourishing Fifties (1950 · 1959)

The economy of the central prairies, already expanding as the decade began, approached a new boom during these years. Prosperity was due in part to Canada's active role in the postwar reconstruction of Europe, in part to favorable weather and good crops, and in part to the discovery of new mineral resources beneath the prairies and up north in the Shield. Potash deposits were first located in 1943, but serious exploration did not begin till the early 1950s, and only in 1956 did mining first begin at Patience Lake east of the city. Within a few years, five mines were operating in the vicinity, and Saskatoon was styling itself "Potash Capital of the World." Since it was closer than Regina, Saskatoon became the supply base for the mines of northern Saskatchewan.

For a second time Saskatoon was one of the fastest growing cities in Canada, its population almost doubling during this decade. However, this time the increase was not so much the result of immigration; rather it was a consequence of the number of "war babies" and of a shift of the population into the city from the rural areas. In the countryside henceforward there would be ever larger farm machinery, larger farms, and fewer farmers.

Construction, especially of housing, flourished, and the city spread once more as new subdivisions arose around its edges. However, since much of this area consisted of land forfeited to the city in default of taxes during the depression, civic control on development was tight and the expansion more orderly. Nevertheless, incomplete services, rutted streets, inadequate schools, and underdeveloped parks were common characteristics both of the old and of the new areas of Saskatoon. In 1955 the town of Sutherland was incorporated into the city, adding to the problems since many of its lots were not serviced.

The university expanded greatly, its new buildings maintaining architectural uniformity. No such harmony was evident in the downtown area. The new structures — the Financial Building, the new City Hall, and the new Hudson's Bay store — were sharply different in style and materials from those buildings surviving from the earlier boomtime. Utilitarian architecture was now in vogue!

Technological changes had a major impact during the fifties. Coal and oil delivery trucks were vanishing as natural gas lines were installed. Mercury lights and neon signs now illuminated the streets. After 1952, television brought the latest news, fashions, popular music, and sports events into most homes.

The factor that had the greatest single impact on the city was, however, the increased availability of motor vehicles. Greater personal mobility changed the lives of businessmen and housewives alike. "Having wheels" became a social necessity for the teenage and college crowds.

Beginning with Grosvenor Park, residential areas were designed to separate pedestrians from traffic. The cenotaph was removed from Twenty-first Street to City Hall to facilitate traffic flow. Traffic lights and parking meters sprouted, and the streetcars were replaced by trolley buses. The first suburban shopping malls (Churchill, Grosvenor Park, and Westgate) were constructed, and along the main highways into the city, lines of motels, drive-in restaurants, and drive-in theatres arose.

Easier travelling and a shorter working week brought more leisure time. Sports flourished. The Hilltop football team, the Quaker hockey club, and the Gem baseball team gained strong support, and golf, curling, swimming, gymnastics, and figure skating were popular. Expanded civic departments found themselves concerned not only with the maintenance of utilities and police and fire protection, but also increasingly with the provision of leisure facilities — parks, rinks, swimming pools, ball diamonds, and branch libraries. Musical, literary, and artistic groups were active, and a natural history society was formed.

In 1955 a branch of the Western Development Museum was established in an old hangar on Eleventh Street. The associated summer show, Pion-Era, soon rivalled the annual exhibition in popularity. The elegantly decorated Capitol Theatre staged a greater-than-ever range of cultural activities. However, the Arena remained the major showplace, housing not only hockey games but also figure skating extravaganzas, the sportsmen's shows, car bingos, carnivals, touring musical shows, and political rallies.

Not all was harmonious in Saskatoon during these years; there were labor strikes and controversies over nuclear armament, liquor laws, socialized medicine, and other matters. Yet, all in all, this was a decade of unprecedented prosperity, leisure, and optimism.

The first National Speed Skating Championship held in Saskatoon (1950), hosted by the local club on the oval in Westview Park.

A temporary "granary." Bumper crops in the region during the 1950s created storage difficulties but stimulated the economy of Saskatoon.

Monument erected in 1952 to the pioneers who established Saskatoon. The dedication of the monument was a prelude to the celebration at the cenotaph, complete with a huge birthday cake, of the seventieth anniversary of the city.

The 406th Light Bomber Squadron, still very active during the 1950s. They were nicknamed the "weekend warriors" because of their regular sessions during the year; their Mitchell bombers took them to camps from Whitehorse to Goose Bay. The squadron was disbanded in 1964.

The 2400 block of York Avenue in the spring of 1950. Impassably rutted streets, outhouses, and water barrels were common in new areas on the fringe of the city.

A member of the Saskatoon Police Force, sheltered from the elements by his buffalo coat, going about his duties. The installation of parking meters in 1952 only added to police responsibilities.

An extra convenience for downtown shoppers. Electrical plug-ins were attached to the parking meters along Twenty-first Street between Second and Third avenues in 1953. Rates were increased from the normal hourly charge of ten cents to fifteen cents on these meters to cover the cost of electricity. The plug-ins were removed a couple of years later because of high maintenance costs.

The summer of 1954. After a cloudburst such as this one, a local radio announcer commented, "... if using the Nineteenth Street subway this morning, I would suggest the backstroke!"

The vicinity of Kilburn Avenue and Second Street. Providing sewer services and water to "unmodern" houses still existing in the mid fifties posed considerable problems, especially in winter.

The first annual Optimist Soap Box Derby down the Avenue H hill, held in the summer of 1952. These races, organized by the Parks and Recreation Department, remained popular throughout the early sixties.

Grosvenor Park, a new development in 1954. Designed by the newly established City Planning Department, it was one of the first subdivisions to provide for a separation of pedestrian and motor traffic.

Prospective buyers of preferred lots in the new Grosvenor Park subdivision waiting in line in the old City Hall, June, 1954.

Hopeful prospects trying out for the Hilltops football club at Kilburn Park in the late summer of 1951, when the team played in the Manitoba-Saskatchewan Junior Football League.

Mayor Sid Buckwold dropping the puck to officially open the Playgrounds Hockey League on December 5, 1958. All minor league games were played on outdoor rinks built or subsidized by the city. The only people who were colder than the players were the parents and friends huddled along the boards.

A Western Canada Hockey League game. Numerous players of local and national note toiled with the senior Quakers during the fifties.

Live broadcasts by western groups such as the Vagabonds, who were sponsored by the Massey-Harris Company, popular in the late forties and fifties.

CFQC-TV, a CBC affiliate. The station broadcast the first television program in Saskatoon on December 5, 1954. For the first couple of years it operated only from early afternoon to midnight. Local programming included Les Edwards with the news, Greg Barnsley's weather report, and "Menu Magic" hosted by Margaret Dallin.

Don Keeler and his orchestra broadcasting on the new CKOM radio station from the Club 400 in the fall of 1951. This popular "night club" in the basement of the Avenue Building sold only soft drinks and ice to its customers.

Relocation of the cenotaph. In the summer of 1957 it was moved from its Twenty-first Street site and re-erected in front of the new City Hall, where the old City Hall had stood.

One of the first carhops in Saskatoon. In 1954 Joe Young built his El Rancho drive-in chicken and hamburger stand on Eighth Street, just east of Preston Avenue. Many considered it a risky venture as it was so far out of town. And after all, who would want to eat in a car!

Eighth Street in the late 1950s. A few years later the El Rancho had been expanded, and other similar outlets, such as the Nighthawk, were being constructed. These businesses gave rise to the ribbon of establishments aimed at highway traffic which characterize Eighth Street today.

The old City Hall — too small to accommodate expanded civic services departments. In 1955 a new, modern City Hall was constructed in the park behind the old one.

Intercontinental Packers, established by Fred Mendel in a former Cordage Park automobile assembly plant in the Eleventh Street industrial area during World War II. The company had grown to become a major employer in Saskatoon during the 1950s.

Playing bingo at the Kinsmen Karnival in 1951. A number of "monster bingos" with large prizes such as cars were held in the Arena during the fifties.

The Saskatchewan Golden Jubilee. Saskatonians took an active part in the celebrations, attending functions such as this square dance in July, 1955.

The new University Hospital. In September, 1952, Premier T. C. Douglas laid the cornerstone. Associated with the medical college, which had been added to the university in 1948, the hospital became the focus of medical care and research in the province.

Aerial view of the University of Saskatchewan. The large open spaces on the university campus were beginning to fill up by 1955. The provincial highway route, which passed through Sutherland and past Griffiths Stadium to College Drive, was unable to handle increased motor traffic. The town of Sutherland was amalgamated with Saskatoon in 1956.

The new airport terminal, completed in 1956. Trans Canada Air Lines offered a regular service, with two North Star aircraft flights each way touching down daily in Saskatoon. The service was an improvement over the single daily flight by unpressurized DC-3s available prior to 1952.

The "Farmers' Market" on Avenue A where No. 1 Fire Hall is now — a busy place on most Saturdays during the fifties.

Her Majesty Queen Elizabeth II and Prince Philip touring the Western Development Museum during the royal visit of 1958. The museum then was housed in an old hangar on Eleventh Street.

The busy intersection at Second Avenue and Twenty-first Street in 1958. Motorists whose cars did not have signal lights were required to signal by hand. The first traffic light in the city had been installed at this intersection in 1946.

"Snake dances" of returning university students, a tradition each fall until 1962, when they were forbidden by the university and civic authorities.

The University Homecoming Parade in the fall of 1959. The expansion of the university community influenced the city socially and politically, as well as economically.

Population changes during the 1950s. The larger proportion of young people in Saskatoon taxed existing recreational facilities. Their diverse free-time activities were largely of their own creation — requiring little organization and limited facilities.

Prime Minister Diefenbaker greeted by local supporters at the CNR station as he hit the campaign trail in 1958. His efforts led to his party's record majority in the House of Commons.

Downtown Saskatoon in 1959, viewed from the northwest. The CPR station is at lower left; the CNR yards are in the center. A major problem was providing access to the city center as the number of private and commercial vehicles converging on it continued to increase.

Chapter 10
The Soaring Sixties (1960 • 1969)

The prosperity of the fifties carried on into the sixties, a decade of steady and confident expansion. Though fluctuations in world market prices and variable rains hurt the prairie agricultural community, the city's economy was buoyed by industrial and university growth and by the developing potash industry. Moreover, during this decade the South Saskatchewan River Project was carried to completion. The building of the largest rolled-earth dam ever constructed in Canada allowed stabilization of the flow of the river, regulation of water supplies, generation of hydroelectric power, and use of the waterway for recreation.

A large industrial district opened up on the city's northwest margin, accommodating mining, maintenance, and service companies. New plants were built by Interprovincial Co-operatives and Armour Chemicals. The H-huts of the No. 7 Flight Training School were cleared from the Avenue A and Thirty-third Street site to make way for the new Saskatchewan (later Kelsey) Technical Institute. Several new buildings were added to the university complex.

By 1966 Saskatoon's population had grown to 115,000. The construction of multiple housing and rental units and the residential development around the city's margins were accelerating. In 1954 the city covered 10,642 acres; by 1966 it covered more than 20,000 acres. As the city grew, so did traffic problems. However, the increasing use of motor vehicles was causing a decline in the use of railways, especially by passengers. Through a 1963 agreement CNR moved its yards out of the city center southwest to Chappell junction.

The railway move opened the way for an "urban facelift" so drastic that ten years later former residents found it hard to recognize the downtown core! Where the station had been there was a huge enclosed shopping mall, Midtown Plaza, centered about a tall office tower and creating a new commercial focus. Adjacent to it were a new YMCA building and the Centennial Auditorium. The Idylwyld freeway and bridge were constructed along the former railway right of way and linked to a widened Avenue A, renamed Idylwyld Drive. Twenty-second Street was carried through the center of the city to preserve a link with the highway entrances from the east (College Drive and Eighth Street). Work began on Circle Drive, designed to enable traffic to bypass the city center entirely as soon as connecting bridges were constructed.

Parks and recreation were given a new priority. A new golf course, campground, lighted fastball park, and football field in Holiday Park helped take pressure off existing facilities. A new baseball park was constructed in front of a racetrack grandstand on the old Pion-Era grounds, replacing the old Cairns Field which was torn down to make way for commercial development along Idylwyld Drive. The Mendel Art Gallery, opened in 1964, gave a new dimension to the artistic life of the city.

However, by the late sixties it was becoming clear that this rate of growth could not continue. Declining world markets for grain and potash, combined with rising costs, brought a slump in local construction. The numbers of apartment vacancies and unsold houses soared. Whereas in the postwar years unemployment had not been a problem, now it was rising.

Throughout North American society, indeed, there was a faltering of confidence. The carefree optimism of the earlier post war years was transformed into a new sense of realism and awareness. In Saskatoon this changing perspective initially was dismissed by many as a mere fad of the young, expressed by clothes and music but without any long-term significance. However, in the years to come, this new attitude would reach out into most sections of the community. Never again would Saskatonians be so lightheartedly confident.

Exhibition attractions. In the fifties and sixties the annual event included the Royal American Shows midway, a grandstand show and afternoon horse races, as well as industrial and agricultural exhibits. The Pioneer Cemetery is located on the river bank just to the right of the tepees in the background.

Governor General Georges Vanier, formally welcomed at the CNR station when he visited Saskatoon in May, 1960. This was the last such official occasion to be held at this central location, for the days of the terminal were numbered.

Awareness of the international nuclear threat, demonstrated in Saskatoon during the late fifties and early sixties. Public protest took on a more local theme during the Medicare controversy in 1962.

The Potash Company of America mine at Patience Lake. The first mine in the province, it had been sunk in the late fifties but experienced flooding until a method of freezing the sediments of the Blairmore Formation was found. The mine came on full stream in the 1960s.

The "last run." A familiar part of the Saskatoon scene disappeared in June, 1962, when the last horse-drawn delivery wagon was replaced by a motorized van.

A hot August afternoon in 1963. Many young Saskatonians converged at the Mayfair Pool. It and Lathey Pool had been constructed in the late 1950s; George Ward Swimming Pool and a number of paddling pools were added during the sixties.

New ventures during the 1960s. A number of small industries such as Western Broom, which made curling brooms, were established in Saskatoon. Many of them received government assistance in an attempt to further diversify the economy of the region.

Gordie Howe taking part in the 1963 official dedication of the football bowl named after him. It is one part of the Holiday Park complex built on the southwest side of the city during the 1960s. The park also includes a campground, golf course, fastball field, and Kinsmen Arena.

The end of an era. The days of the steam locomotives with their characteristic funnel of smoke, chugging noise, and eerie whistle finally ended in 1960. Diesels had been slowly replacing the steam locomotives since the early 1950s.

The last train to pass over the CNR bridge out of the downtown yards in November, 1964, before workmen began tearing it down as part of a relocation project. The Rail-liner was a single-unit passenger vehicle. It was introduced in 1951 to provide economic daily passenger service from Prince Albert to Regina when regular passenger trains were no longer warranted because of declining demand.

The new CNR yard located at Chappell junction southwest of the city, officially opened in the summer of 1964.

Fall, 1966. The Centennial Auditorium and the CN Tower were under construction behind the former CNR station, which was demolished shortly after. The multi-million dollar complex was also to include the Midtown Plaza.

The Idylwyld Bridge and freeway, taking shape at the same time on the right of way of the original railway line through Saskatoon. Attempts to use the piers of the railway bridge for a new traffic bridge proved unsatisfactory, and they had to be blasted out of the way before the new bridge could be constructed.

Detours and delays, common during the sixties. Several main traffic routes such as Twenty-second Street, shown here in 1962, were widened, and new corridors were constructed through the former central CNR rail yards.

The Mendel Art Gallery, constructed on a scenic river bank site in 1964. It is named after a local industrialist who helped pay the cost of the building and donated a collection of Canadian paintings. An auditorium, intended for piano recitals and small theatrical productions, and a glass-enclosed plant conservatory were part of the complex from the beginning.

The entrance to the Pion-Era grounds on Eleventh Street during the 1965 show.

"Doc" Harry Landa toasting dancing girls in the Blue Garter Saloon during the 1965 Pion-Era show.

The saskatoon berry pie-eating contest, a popular event at the Pion-Era show during the 1960s.

Numerous additions to the university campus to accommodate an increasing enrolment, which was over 8,000 in 1965. These included the Arts Building, Marquis Hall, and the law-commerce complex.

The old Public Library and Fire Hall on Third Avenue and Twenty-third Street. They were demolished in 1966, and a new, larger Public Library was erected on the site. A new No. 1 Fire Hall had been constructed on the site of the old Farmers' Market on Avenue A (Idylwyld Drive) in 1964.

A view of suburban development, showing Greystone Heights and Brevoort Park in the mid 1960s. Planned subdivisions were being built up on all sides of the city. Businesses like drive-in theatres, eateries, and motor hotels continued to be established along highway entrances.

City Hall, decorated in preparation for the July 1 Canadian centennial celebration in 1967.

Saskatoon, "The City of Bridges," in 1968. Because of increased demands for space, high-rises and parkades were invading former residential streets in the central core of the city by the late sixties.

Chapter 11
The Speculative Seventies (1970·1979)

In a decade when economic crises of global scale transmitted their shock waves throughout Canada, Saskatchewan could not escape the effects of recession. The energy crises and the consequent inordinate increases in the costs, not just of fuel but of food, manufactured goods, and services, caused labor strikes and business failures. Nevertheless, it was a period that wrought further marked changes to the face of Saskatoon — some for the better, some for the worse.

Local initiative and help from senior levels of government brought a number of new industries to the city — GWG and Westcott clothing manufacturers, SED Systems, Northern Telecom, and others. Expanded steel manufacturing plants and a new sewage treatment plant were established on the northern fringe. New shopping centers, motels, and food outlets continued to be constructed, especially along the highway entrances. A major addition to the airport, completed in 1975, enabled the handling of increased traffic and freight, and a new Saskatchewan Transportation Company bus depot was opened. The new courthouse was complemented by the building of a new central police station and the opening of two new penal institutions.

On the university campus, a new education building, a radiology laboratory, a dentistry building, and major additions to the University Hospital were completed. Additions to the engineering building and the Western College of Veterinary Medicine were begun. Place Riel provided a sorely needed center for the growing student population.

Mining was becoming increasingly important to the city's economy. During the late seventies Saskatoon was chosen as headquarters for the new Potash Corporation of Saskatchewan. Plans were made for developing the heavy oil deposits of the province. Construction of a uranium refinery near Warman seemed certain.

All this development precipitated a flurry of construction downtown. Office buildings and residential high-rises arose from the sites of demolished older buildings. The Standard Trust Building went, to make way for the modernistic Sturdy-Stone

Centre. The old King Edward School was levelled following a fire, and numerous lesser buildings vanished almost overnight. The streets of the city core began to be the concrete-and-glass canyons so typical of modern urban centers. Saddest of the losses were the unique Capitol Theatre and the adjacent Bank of Nova Scotia, torn down almost overnight in 1979. Three years later, their site is still empty.

A new factor in the city's life was the rise of community and neighborhood organizations, such as the Saskatoon Environmental Society, aimed at exerting pressures on all levels of government — federal, provincial, and civic. Popular opposition to specific projects, including a riverside housing development, the destruction of the Capitol Theatre, and the Warman uranium refinery, provided impetus to the growth of these organizations.

One outcome of this general concern for the urban environment was the creation of the Meewasin Valley Authority by the city, the University of Saskatchewan, the Rural Municipality of Corman Park, and the provincial government. The ward system, reimposed by the provincial government in 1976, provided direct aldermanic representation of particular districts.

Sport and recreation continued to be major concerns. An artificial ski hill was constructed at Blackstrap coulee south of the city in 1971, the year that Saskatoon hosted the Canada Winter Games. Five years later, the new Field House was hurriedly completed for the Western Canada Summer Games. Once construction problems were overcome, it provided welcome accommodation for track clubs hitherto forced to practise in the underground parking lot of Midtown Plaza during inclement weather.

Three FM radio stations, a second television station, and two new weekly community newspapers were established, while the installation of cable television made available a wider range of broadcasting channels. Live theatre gained new prominence. Vigorous groups supported opera, the Saskatoon Symphony Orchestra, jazz, and folk music and dance. The Ukrainian Yevshan Ballet attained international renown. The new Western Development Museum was opened adjacent to the Exhibition Grounds. The name of the summer show at the Exhibition Grounds, known for a time as Saskachimo Exposition, was changed to "Pioneer Days" — the theme of the former Pion-Era show which had been discontinued after 1969.

Saskatoon's population continued to climb during this decade, not only through the migration away from rural areas but also because of the new developments; by the end of 1979, it stood at 147,354. Land values increased faster than the rate of inflation. Though some promises remained unfulfilled, by the end of the decade there had been much solid achievement.

The annual Louis Riel Day Race, started in the seventies and now a highlight of the days preceding exhibition week each summer.

World ski champion Nancy Green Raine, who officiated at the opening of Mount Blackstrap and the skiing events of the Canada Winter Games held in Saskatoon during February, 1971.

Straw being blown onto Blackstrap ski hill in an attempt to trap snow and provide a base during the early seventies before snow-making equipment was obtained.

Labor strife in the construction and service industries, a feature of the Saskatoon scene during the 1970s. The photograph shows the lineup outside the Liquor Board Store on First Avenue to make purchases after the ending of a strike.

Strange modes of transportation at the corner of Cumberland and Main following a cloudburst in June, 1970.

The last trolley bus making a stop on the last run before being taken out of service, May 10, 1974. The trolley buses were replaced by diesel-powered buses which, at the time, were as cheap to operate and allowed more flexible routing.

The Gordie Howe ball field, the site of exciting fastball action. Names like the Merchants and Imperials became very familiar in the early seventies when these senior men's and women's fastball teams won national championships.

Super stocks in action at the Saskatoon International Raceway, south of Saskatoon, in July, 1974. Motor racing of all forms — stock cars, dirt bikes, and even go-carts — took on a new popularity during the 1970s.

Engineers using their grapefruit cannon to draw attention to the 1971 United Appeal Campaign on the university campus.

Pedalling "10 speeds" for health and enjoyment in the downtown area, May, 1972.

"Saskachimo," a new name for the summer show. It was chosen in 1971 from entries in a public contest and revealed in a glamorous fashion. The name was changed to "Pioneer Days" in the late seventies. The theme of the Pion-Era show, associated with the old Western Development Museum on Eleventh Street, was adopted by the exhibition after the new Western Development Museum was constructed on the Exhibition Grounds in 1972.

A warm summer afternoon at Pike Lake, 1974. This small lake, only a short drive from the city, has been a popular weekend recreational site since the 1950s.

"Participaction," a well known slogan of the seventies. A fitness campaign begun in Saskatoon in 1971 included the Block Walk during February, 1973. Local residents logged a greater distance walked or jogged than the citizens of Umeå, Sweden.

Looking north on Second Avenue in 1973. This wide roadway had undergone many changes over the years. About 1968 an overhead walkway was constructed between the Hudson's Bay department store and the parkade across the street.

Another example of a new accent on outdoor recreation and health. During the mid seventies a skating rink was poured in front of City Hall each winter.

In keeping with the more active role taken by women. The first female recruit was added to the Saskatoon city police force in 1973.

Action on the temporary wooden track at the Arena. Despite the limitations of existing facilities, track and field took on new popularity during the 1970s because of indoor competitions and the achievements of local athletes such as Diane Jones, shown here competing in the senior women's high jump competition during the 1970 Knights of Columbus Indoor Games. John Konihowski of the University of Saskatchewan carried the baton for the final leg of the 4 x 4 400-meter invitational relay in the 1972 Knights of Columbus Indoor Games.

Public demonstration in May, 1979. On the fiftieth anniversary of the Capitol Theatre, local community action groups held a "birthday party" to protest plans for demolition of the theatre, but to little avail, for it came under the wrecking ball later that year.

Professional theatrical groups in Saskatoon. Formed during the early 1970s, the companies staged local productions in a number of different temporary facilities. Here the cast of the 25th Street Theatre's nationally acclaimed "Paper Wheat" are congratulated on the set after a sellout performance in Castle Theatre at Aden Bowman Collegiate, June, 1979.

The river banks, the focus of recreation, threatened by commercial development with continued growth of the city. In 1979 the Meewasin Valley Authority was formally established to coordinate and direct development along the South Saskatchewan River Valley through the Saskatoon district.

Landscape architect Raymond Moriyama consulting with local civic groups during the preparation of a "Hundred Year Master Plan" for the Meewasin Valley Authority.

Evidence of a modern land rush, which developed when lots in River Heights were made available in the early seventies. Citizens camped in tents on the lawn in front of City Hall to assure their place in line for the allocation of lots.

Major renovations made to the "Diamond" intersection at Thirty-third Street and Warman Road in 1972. This intersection had been the scene of some of the worst traffic accidents in the city's history.

The Field House, hurriedly completed on the university campus to host the Western Canada Summer Games held in Saskatoon in 1979. This facility enabled a much wider range of year-round track and field events, as well as a range of other athletic activities such as tennis, gymnastics, and boxing.

A view down University Drive during the early seventies. An attractive feature of Saskatoon is its tree-lined boulevards, a result of the earlier civic policy of planting trees in new areas as soon as they were developed.

A gathering of dignitaries from across the country. The bodies of former Prime Minister John G. Diefenbaker and his wife Olive were interred with pomp and ceremony in front of the Diefenbaker Centre on the university campus, August 22, 1979.

Chapter 12
Entering the Eighties

The last two years of Saskatoon's first century have brought further changes to the cityscape. More and more high-rises are sprouting in the city center, though more slowly now following the increase in interest rates and a slowdown in resource development. Today comparatively few older buildings survive downtown. Some of these have been tastefully refurbished, including the MacMillan Building, two of the Drinkle blocks, the Avalon Building (Thompson Chambers), and the Oddfellows Hall. A beginning has also been made on civic designation of historic buildings.

Construction of the Forty-second Street Bridge and its approach is nearing completion. The new Ukrainian Museum of Canada opened on the river bank in 1980, and the construction of a major arts/museum/theatre complex on Twenty-fifth Street is under consideration. Plans are being made to replace the Arena, now nicknamed "the old barn," with a larger multifunctional complex. On the university campus, the veterinary college and engineering additions are almost completed, and a geology building is planned.

Under the aegis of the Meewasin Valley Authority, a prehistoric park is to be developed centered on Tipperary Creek, and new parks and pathways are to be provided on both banks of the river. The Authority and the city are formulating joint plans for the redevelopment of the riverside adjacent to the downtown business district. The years ahead promise to be exciting.

As Saskatoon enters its second century, its citizens inevitably must recall the years of optimism, hardship, growth, and change that past generations have experienced. Yet their aspirations parallel those of the founding fathers — to maintain a wholesome community astride the South Saskatchewan River, in a land of "prosperity, peace, and plenty," for themselves and their children.

An outdoor "Farmers' Market." It operated on Saturday mornings during the summer months behind City Hall. It is now held in the street between City Hall and the Public Library.

Volunteers helping young people relive life on the prairies at the turn of the century by guiding them down "Mainstreet" of "Boomtown" at the Western Development Museum. This large indoor complex was opened on the Exhibition Grounds in 1972.

The Saskatoon Airport, 1980. An enlarged terminal which facilitated the movement of an increasing volume of passengers and air freight to and from the city had been completed. Four carriers were offering up to eighteen flights through Saskatoon daily at that time, and a fifth was added in 1982.

The south end of Fourth Avenue taking on a new form in 1980, bringing back memories of the construction of Third Avenue during the pre-World War I boom.

The central area of Saskatoon in 1981. Green spaces and private residences have almost disappeared, while Midtown Plaza, presently being enlarged, has become the commercial focus of the city.

High-rise apartment buildings had arisen alongside Nutana Collegiate (left) on the east bank of the river by 1980. The Meewasin Valley Authority is planning improvements in the recreational use of the river bank parks.

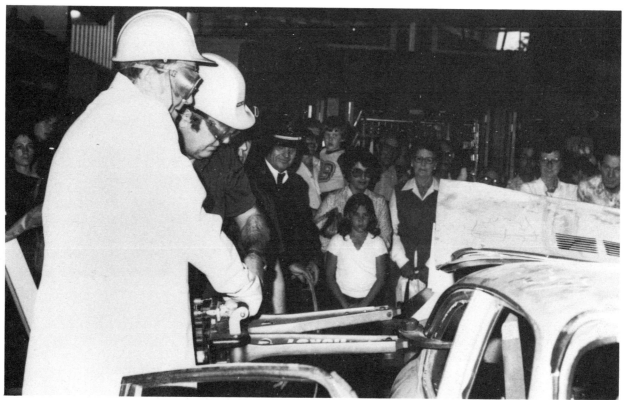

Mayor Wright apparently enjoying the performance of his civic duties. Here he is using the "jaws of life" device at a fire department display at Midtown Plaza.

The piers and abutments of the new Forty-second Street Bridge, constructed by January, 1982. Completion of the bridge, scheduled for 1984, will bring the Circle Drive bypass, begun in the 1960s, closer to completion.

The Saskatoon skyline, 1980. Continued construction of high-rises had reduced the dominance the Bessborough had maintained for almost five decades.

Lakeview, a unique subdivision developed in the early 1980s and planned around a man-made lake in southeast Nutana. A group of Evan Hardy Collegiate students is seen using the lake for an outdoor education class.

Obviously exuberant Holy Cross Crusaders after winning the 1981 4A high school football championship. They defeated the Mount Royal Mustangs. Bedford Road and City Park collegiates dominated the league until the late 1960s, when they were supplanted by the newer schools such as Aden Bowman and then Evan Hardy and Holy Cross in more recent years.

A view of Saskatoon from the northeast in 1981. The little settlement established on the banks of the meandering South Saskatchewan River almost a century earlier had grown considerably.

New Year's Eve, 1981. Centennial year celebrations began with a giant "birthday party" at the Auditorium. At midnight Special Reasons, a musical group formed specifically for this anniversary year, reflected on why Saskatonians should be thankful for past blessings and a bright future.

Picture Credits

The following abbreviations are used to indicate photograph sources:

LHR   Local History Room, Saskatoon Public Library

SAB   Saskatchewan Archives Board

SAB-*SP*   Saskatchewan Archives Board, *Star-Phoenix* Collection

SP   Saskatoon *Star-Phoenix, Star-Phoenix* photo

1. The Centuries before Saskatoon (to 1882)

P 3., *SP*
P. 4, top, Saskatchewan Museum of Natural History
P. 4, bottom, LHR
P. 5, top and bottom, LHR

2. The Temperance Colony Era (1882 · 1903)

P. 8, SAB, (TCS) (2)
P. 8, insert, W. P. Delainey and W. A. S. Sarjeant
P. 9, top left, Morton (ed.), *Narratives of Saskatoon* (Saskatoon: University of Saskatchewan Bookstore, 1927), frontispiece
P. 9 top right, Royal Canadian Mounted Police Museum, Regina
P. 9, bottom, SAB
P. 10, top, SAB, RA 7438(a)
P. 10, bottom, Peel and Knowles, *The Saskatoon Story*
(Saskatoon: M. A. East, 1952), p. 20
P. 11, top left, SAB
P. 11, top right and bottom, LHR
P. 12, top and bottom, LHR
P. 13, top and bottom, LHR
P. 14, top, SAB, RA 2328
P. 14, bottom, LHR
P. 15, top and bottom, LHR
P. 16, LHR
P. 17, top and bottom, LHR

3. Three Settlements Become a City (1903 · 1907)

P. 19, SAB, RA 4586
P. 20, top, SAB, RA 4587
P. 20, bottom, SAB, RA 2309
P. 21, top and bottom, LHR
P. 22, top and bottom, LHR
P. 23, top, SAB, RB 806
P. 23, bottom, LHR
P. 24, LHR
P. 25, top, LHR
P. 25, bottom, LHR, donated by A. Needham
P. 26, top and bottom, LHR
P. 27, top, W. P. Delainey and W. A. S. Sarjeant
P. 27, bottom, LHR
P. 28, LHR
P. 29, top, SAB, RB 9364
P. 29, bottom, LHR
P. 30, top, LHR
P. 30, bottom, SAB, RB 3710
P. 31, LHR
P. 32, LHR
P. 33, top, LHR
P. 33, bottom, SAB, RB 205(2)
P. 34, LHR

4. The Boom Years (1908 · 1914)

P. 36, LHR
P. 37, top, SAB, RA 2313
P. 37, bottom, Glenbow Archives, NA-387-5
P. 38, top and bottom, LHR
P. 39, top and bottom, LHR
P. 40, LHR
P. 41, top, SAB, RA 2366
P. 41, bottom, SAB, RA 519
P. 42, LHR
P. 43, top and bottom, LHR
P. 44, top and bottom, LHR
P. 45, top and bottom, LHR
P. 46, top and bottom, LHR
P. 47, top and bottom, LHR
P. 48, top and bottom, LHR
P. 49, top and bottom, LHR
P. 50, LHR
P. 51, top and bottom, LHR
P. 52, LHR
P. 53, top and bottom, LHR
P. 54, top, SAB, RA 7654
P. 54, bottom, LHR
P. 55, LHR
P. 56, top and bottom, LHR
P. 57, LHR
P. 58, top and bottom, LHR
P. 59, LHR

5.Years of the Great War (1914·1918)

P. 61, top, LHR
P. 61, bottom, SAB, RA 233(1)
P. 62, top, Royal Canadian Legion #63, Saskatoon
P. 62, bottom, SAB, RA 217(1)
P. 63, top left, Diefenbaker Centre, University of Saskatchewan, J.G.D.-62
P. 63, top right, LHR
P. 63, bottom, Western Development Museum, Saskatoon

P. 64, top, SAB, RB 977
P. 64, bottom, SAB, RB 9269
P. 65, SAB, RB 177
P. 66, LHR
P. 67, top, SAB, RB 3436
P. 67, bottom, SAB, RB 2238
P. 68, top, LHR
P. 68, bottom left and right, *65th Gazette*, vol. 1, no. 24, May 31, 1916

6.Prosperity Regained (1919·1929)

P. 70, top and bottom, LHR
P. 71, top and bottom, LHR
P. 72, top, SAB, RB 3074(3)
P. 72, bottom, LHR
P. 73, CFQC Radio, Saskatoon
P. 74, CFQC Radio, Saskatoon
P. 75, top, SAB, RB 2245c.2
P. 75, bottom, Gibson Photos
P. 76, top, LHR
P. 76, bottom, LHR, Hillyard Collection
P. 77, top and bottom, Saskatoon Golf and Country Club
P. 78, top, LHR
P. 78, bottom, Gibson Photos

P. 79, top and bottom, Gibson Photos
P. 80, top, SAB, RB 2237
P. 80, bottom, LHR
P. 81, LHR
P. 82, top, LHR
P. 82, bottom, Walter West
P. 83, LHR, Hillyard and Gibson
P. 84, LHR, Hillyard and Gibson
P. 85, top, Gibson Photos
P. 85, bottom, Ukrainian Museum of Canada, 973-70
P. 86, top, Glenbow Archives, NA-2256-13
P. 86, bottom, LHR
P. 87, Glenbow Archives, NE-3-310

7.Dust and Depression (1929·1939)

P. 89, Gibson Photos
P. 90, top, SAB, RB 772(3)
P. 90, bottom, LHR
P. 91, LHR, Hillyard Collection
P. 92, top, LHR
P. 92, bottom, Soils Department, University of Saskatchewan
P. 93, LHR
P. 94, top, LHR
P. 94, bottom, University of Saskatchewan Archives
P. 95, top, Glenbow Archives, ND-3-6742
P. 95, bottom, Saskatoon Arena, Hillyard Collection

P. 96, top, Norm Robson
P. 96, bottom, Gibson Photos
P. 97, Gibson Photos
P. 98, top, Gibson Photos
P. 98, bottom, SAB, RB 1408
P. 99, top, Gibson Photos
P. 99, bottom, LHR
P. 100, top, Gibson Photos
P. 100, bottom, Hugh Cairns VC Armoury, Hillyard Collection
P. 101, Hugh Cairns VC Armoury, Hillyard Collection

8.The Second World War and Its Aftermath (1939·1949)

P. 103, LHR
P. 104, top, Hugh Cairns VC Armoury
P. 104, bottom, LHR, Hillyard Collection
P. 105, top, LHR, Hillyard Collection
P. 105, bottom, LHR
P. 106, top, Gibson Photos
P. 106, bottom, SAB, RA 9064
P. 107, top, Marion Graham
P. 107, bottom, LHR, Hillyard Collection
P. 108, LHR

P. 109, top and bottom, LHR
P. 110, Hugh Cairns VC Armoury
P. 111, Modern Press, Hillyard Collection
P. 112, Parks and Recreation Department, Saskatoon, *Star-Phoenix* photo
P. 113, top and bottom, SAB-*SP*
P. 114, top, LHR, Hillyard Collection
P. 114, bottom, SAB-*SP*
P. 115, LHR, Hillyard Collection

9.The Flourishing Fifties (1950·1959)

P. 117, top, *SP*

P. 117, bottom, SAB-*SP*, SP-B899(5)

P. 118, top, SAB-*SP*, SP-B1500(21)

P. 118, bottom, SAB-*SP*, SP-B146(7)

P. 119, top, Marion Graham

P. 119, bottom, SAB-*SP*, SP-B462(2)

P. 120, top, SAB-*SP*, SP-B2460(2)

P. 120, bottom, SAB-*SP*, SP-B525(1)

P. 121, top left, SAB-*SP*, SP-B3009(20)

P. 121, top right, SAB-*SP*, SP-B3752(14)

P. 121, bottom, SAB-*SP*, SP-B846(1)

P. 122, top, LHR

P. 122, bottom, SAB-*SP*, SP-B2787(2)

P. 123, top, SAB-*SP*, SP-B825(2)

P. 123, bottom, SAB-*SP*, SP-B6872(4)

P. 124, top, Saskatoon Arena, *Star-Phoenix* photo

P. 124, bottom, CFQC Radio, Saskatoon

P. 125, top, CFQC-TV, Saskatoon

P. 125, bottom, LHR, Hillyard Collection

P. 126, top left, SAB-*SP*, SP-B4382(1)

P. 126, top right and bottom, Joe Young, El-Rancho Food Services Limited

P. 127, top, LHR

P. 127, bottom, LHR, Hillyard Collection

P. 128, top, SAB-*SP*, SP-B704(3)

P. 128, bottom, SAB-*SP*, SP-B3548(1)

P. 129, top, University Hospital Archives, Hillyard Collection

P. 129, bottom, LHR, Hillyard Collection

P. 130, top and bottom, LHR

P. 131, top and bottom, LHR, Hillyard Collection

P. 132, top, SAB-*SP*, SP-B2372(5)

P. 132, bottom, SAB-*SP*, SP-B188(10)

P. 133, top left, SAB-*SP*, SP-B4050(2)

P. 133, top right, SAB-*SP*, SP-B6974(1)

P. 133, bottom, SAB-*SP*, SP-B3187(1)

P. 134, top, SAB, RB 1882(1)

P. 134, bottom, LHR, Hillyard Collection

10.The Soaring Sixties (1960·1969)

P. 136, LHR, Hillyard Collection

P. 137, top, SAB-*SP*, SP-B5129(8)

P. 137, bottom, SAB-*SP*, SP-B2724(1)

P. 138, top, Creative Professional Photographers Ltd.

P. 138, bottom, LHR

P. 139, top left, Parks and Recreation Department, Saskatoon

P. 139, top right, SAB, RB 5541(3)

P. 139, bottom, CFQC-TV, Saskatoon

P. 140, top left, SAB-*SP*, SP-B5483(1)

P. 140, top right, SAB-*SP*, SP-B5864(2)

P. 140, bottom, SAB–*SP*, SP-B5902(5)

P. 141, top, SAB, Lumby Productions Collection, 139(2)

P. 141, bottom, LHR

P. 142, top, SAB-*SP*, SP-B5019(1)

P. 142, bottom, LHR, Hillyard Collection

P. 143, top left, top right, and bottom, Delmar Studios Ltd.

P. 144, top, LHR

P. 144, bottom, LHR, Creative Professional Photographers Ltd.

P. 145, top, LHR, Hillyard Collection

P. 145, bottom, LHR, Creative Professional Photographers Ltd.

P. 146, LHR, Creative Professional Photographers Ltd.

11.The Speculative Seventies (1970·1979)

P. 148, top and bottom, *SP*

P. 149, top, *SP*

P. 149, bottom, SAB-*SP*, SP-A7164(3)

P. 150, top, SAB-*SP*, SP-B6111(2)

P. 150, bottom, M. A. Wilson

P. 151, top, SAB-*SP*, SP-B6136(1)

P. 151, bottom, SAB-*SP*, SP-A7136(11)

P. 152, top, W. P. Delainey

P. 152, bottom, *SP*

P. 153, top, *SP*

P. 153, bottom, SAB-*SP*

P. 154, top, SAB-*SP*

P. 154, bottom, W. P. Delainey, Project Canada West Collection

P. 155, top, SAB-*SP*, SP-A6601(12)

P. 155, bottom, SAB-*SP*

P. 156, top and bottom, Lyle Sanderson, University of Saskatchewan

P. 157, top, Billy Walker

P. 157, bottom, 25th Street Theatre, Patrick Close photo

P. 158, *SP*

P. 159, top, Meewasin Valley Authority

P. 159, bottom, John D. Duerkop

P. 160, top, SAB-*SP*, SP-B7203(20)

P. 160, bottom, *SP*

P. 161, top, W. A. S. Sarjeant

P. 161, bottom, *SP*

12. Entering the Eighties

P. 162, *SP*

P. 163, top and bottom, *SP*

P. 164, top and bottom, *SP*

P. 165, top, W. A. S. Sarjeant

P. 165, bottom, Saskatoon Fire Department

P. 166, top, Barb Butler photo

P. 166, bottom, *SP*

P. 167, top and bottom, Cairns Homes

P. 168, top, John Perret

P. 168, bottom, W. A. S. Sarjeant

P. 169, *SP*

Index